BOATS *MADE IN*
HOLLAND

BOATS MADE IN HOLLAND

· A Michigan Tradition ·

GEOFFREY D. REYNOLDS

THE
History
PRESS

Published by The History Press
Charleston, SC
www.historypress.com

Copyright © 2018 by Geoffrey D. Reynolds
All rights reserved

Front cover, bottom image courtesy of Mac Bay Boat Company Collection. Back cover, top images courtesy of the Roger MacLeod Collection, Holland Museum Archives and Research Library.

First published 2018

Manufactured in the United States

ISBN 9781467135337

Library of Congress Control Number: 2017963918

Much love to you, always, Jennifer, Hannah and Peter.

CONTENTS

PREFACE

T his book was inspired by a need to learn as much as I could about a long-standing and vibrant industry which had largely been forgotten by the Holland, Michigan history community. My focus was primarily on the stock boat builders of the area. I do include small builders, as they also played important roles in the development of the boat building industry. The companies included in this book include the following:

- Beacon Boat Company (1953–60)
- Campbell Boat Company (1937–56)
- Chris-Craft Corporation/Chris-Craft Industries/Murray Chris-Craft (1939–89)
- Gill-Boat Company (1934–42)
- Grand Craft Corporation/Grand-Craft Acquisitions, LLC/ Grand Craft Boats (1979–present)
- Holland Launch and Engine Company (1907–16)
- Jesiek Brothers (1910–73)
- Lovecraft (1970–72)
- Mac Bay Boat Company (1948–56)
- Michigan Fiberglass Company/Plastics Inc. (1960–63)
- Poll Manufacturing (1954–60)
- Power Play Boat Company/PowerQuest Inc. (1983–2005)
- PQ Marine Holdings (2007–11)
- Roamer Boat Company (1946–55)

- Roamer Yachts Division of Chris-Craft Corporation/Chris-Craft Industries (1955–79)
- Skipper-Craft Boats (1952–60)
- Slick Craft Boat Company (1954–69)
- Slickcraft Division of AMF Corporation (1969–80)
- S2 Yachts Inc. (S2 Sailboats, Tiara Slickcraft, SlickCraft, Tiara Yachts, Pursuit) (1974–present)
- Victory Shipbuilding Company (1942–45)
- Westease/New Holland Marine (1985–present)
- Wolverine Motor Works (1901–7)

Companies not included:

- Bow Winds Boats Inc. (1987–89)
- Cam-Per Craft Boat Building Corporation (1942–45)
- Clark, George Edward (1895–97)
- Dutch Craft Boat Works (1931)
- Ensign Boat Company (1946–48)
- Glen Eddy Company (1960–66)
- Holland Boat Manufacturing Company (1930)
- Inland Boat Service (Ken Craft boats) (circa 1950s and 1960s)
- Mac Bay Boat Company (Muskegon, 1955–62)
- Moes Enterprise (1983–90)
- Ottawa Pleasure Boat & Yawl Building Company (1893)
- Powerboats Inc. (1960–61)

More information about all companies is located at http://boatsmadeinhollandmichigan.org.

As a historian new to the community in 1997 and looking to research a subject relating to the Holland area, I soon discovered a whole new set of resources not typically found in archival collections or even sourced by authors writing on the subject. Those new sources included industry-specific and popular boating magazines, company brochures, local directories, maps, oral histories conducted and written down during the early twentieth century by other historians, diaries, letters, newspaper articles, corporate annual reports, state and federal censuses and company records. Together, these sources help me understand relationships within this local industry and how important they were for its success, both locally and nationwide. Even with those sources, I knew I was still missing small and short-lived companies, so I set out to locate local boat builders and interview them as a formal oral history project in 2001—and I continue to do so today. At the present time, almost one hundred oral histories have been conducted. Sometimes these oral histories provide the only evidence that a boat builder had even existed. Many times, these interviews caused me to revisit and search deeper into the sources to discover new information.

ACKNOWLEDGEMENTS

Like any history book, there were many people involved at many levels to make it a success. I am thankful for those who encouraged me to write this book, helped with research materials, provided helpful writing advice and helped make it look like a book.

From the beginning, Scott Peters of the State of Michigan Museum encouraged me to tell the story of the Holland area boat builders as he was writing his book, *Making Waves: Michigan's Boat-Building Industry, 1865–2000.* Many pieces came together through collaboration. The impetus for this book came largely from an exhibit I curated for the Holland Museum in 2013, as well as a small Hope College writing group I was part of, along with Dr. Curtis Gruenler and Dr. David Cunningham. Curtis and David were very supportive of my desire to complete the museum exhibit and continue the momentum with a published book. Thank you both.

Another major source of encouragement came from my parents, Douglas and Betsy Reynolds, who have always supported my dream of working with history as a profession and sharing my research through writing and presenting. I also wish to thank the very people who built the boats, large and small. By documenting their stories through their oral histories, I was not only able to find inspiration to continue my research but also place their experiences within the research community's reach for the first time. While many of them have passed, their stories will live on through this book and at the Joint Archives of Holland, Hope College. Other experts in the field who were willing to share their resources and expertise include Stan Grayson, C. Patrick Labadie, Robert Graham, Jim and Norm Wangard, Lee Wangstad, Thomas Holmes, Rick Jenkins at the Holland Museum and many unnamed others.

To my acquisition editors, Krista Slavicek and Candice Lawrence; copy editor Ryan Finn; and the staff at The History Press, I thank you for giving me the opportunity to present my research and writing through the organization and publishing of this book. Thank you for partnering with me to make a dream a reality.

To my two wonderful and understanding children, Hannah and Peter Reynolds, thank you for listening to my endless stories of local boat builders and understanding why it was important to tell their stories to you as well as to the world. Lastly, to my manuscript editor and lovely, intelligent and patient wife, Jennifer Uehlein Reynolds, I thank you for your endless patience with my writing and helping me turn my research into a readable document that others might enjoy. Much love to you, always, Jennifer, Hannah and Peter.

INTRODUCTION

*B*oats Made in Holland: A Michigan Tradition features the men and women who produced watercraft with creativity, skillful hands, financial resources and cooperation. It also illustrates the area's rich and long history of successful companies, both large and small, that produced pleasure boats, working boats and military craft. Companies succeeded by working together toward a common goal, maintaining spiritual practices and commitment to family.

The story behind the success of watercraft building in the area starts with the people who created each and every design. From the very beginning, builders of small pleasure craft began to market their products to local resort owners so their guests could enjoy the nearby lakes. At the beginning of the twentieth century, local craftsmen constructed pleasure craft with marine engines to give passengers a less strenuous day on the lake. Many such artisans, eager to become successful entrepreneurs, created pleasure, military and work vessels from wood, steel, aluminum and fiberglass. Most eventually failed because of death, disease, disintegration of family or debt in changing economic times.

The Holland area has benefited from the creation of many small boat building enterprises, starting in the 1940s and continuing through today. One such firm began building and selling cabin cruisers made of steel sheets welded together and became so successful that the huge Chris-Craft Corporation purchased the company in 1955 to fill out its line of cruisers. Others, based in the furniture industry, began making wooden boats crafted from inexpensive and sturdy sheet and molded plywood hulls purchased from nearby Grand Rapids. In the late 1950s, a new boat building medium splashed onto the scene: Fiberglass Reinforced Plastic (FRP). This new medium, first invented in the 1930s and used successfully by the United States military during World War II, completely changed boat building.

From the very beginning of boat building in Holland, family has played a key role in the success or failure of the individual shipyard or boat factory. Families came to Holland as boat builders from the Netherlands in the 1840s and built flatboats and ships for local merchants until they grew too old for the work or left for other opportunities. Large and small companies started with husbands and wives who had dreams to make boats designed by their tastes, built by their hands and sold via their relationships with others. Many of these families disintegrated from the stress of making and losing money, time away from one another and the loss of confidence. A few stuck to ideals, even during the worst of times, and persevered with attention to their spiritual life and being accountable to their coworkers, customers and themselves.

For many years, the workforce in local boat factories was largely made up of Dutch woodworkers and farmers. After World War II, laborers of all ethnic backgrounds made their way to Holland for temporary work and decided to stay where a strong work ethic, family values and spirituality were encouraged. As larger workforces were needed in the boat factories, immigrants to our community were able to find positions there, as were their children.

Much like the history of industry around the nation, as boat craftsmen in small shops competed with larger firms, they lost a share of the market, which reduced hundreds of small companies to just a few conglomerates today. Their personal stories demonstrate how difficult it was to be successful for long periods of time, especially when faced with fluctuating economic cycles and lack of financial resources. The purpose of this book is to relate the stories of their innovation, struggles and achievements and provide the reader with an understanding of one of Holland, Michigan's largest local industries along with a sense of the industrious spirit that helped create their community.

Chapter I

SMALL CRAFT SHOPS

S purred by a technological advance in motive power in 1883, first naphtha-, then gasoline engine–powered wooden launches replaced the lagging shipbuilding industry in the Holland area, and local craftsmen at small craft shops built those boats for consumers from around the world.[1] But this new style of pleasure craft would not last long. By the 1920s, wooden launches were considered too slow for a speed-hungry consumer enjoying faster cars, some called "runabouts," on land and reading about aquatic daredevils like Gar Wood steadily approaching one hundred miles per hour on water. That trend ended business for many local boat building shops, while new ones were established using larger and more reliable engines to power fast hydroplanes, speedboats and cruisers. Other small craft shops opened up on Lake Macatawa and built large and small wind- and gasoline-powered wooden and steel boats for consumers for recreational use, as well as for the United States government's military use.

WOLVERINE MOTOR WORKS

The Sintz Gas Engine Company was established on Canal Street in Grand Rapids, Michigan, in December 1892 by Clark Sintz to manufacture stationary and marine gasoline engines for boats and launches.[2] The September 30, 1893 issue of *Scientific American* spotlighted the company

Launch *Knickerbocker* on Black Lake, circa 1900. *Sears Riepma Collection.*

for its innovations in gasoline engine design, landing it a spot in the 1893 World's Columbian Exposition. The next year, advertisements in Northern Michigan periodicals illustrated the fact that the company was building boats as well as engines.[3] In 1894, the stockholders of the company voted to increase the capital stock of the corporation from $30,000 to $100,000 to increase production of both gasoline engines and boats.[4] By 1895, the company had changed its name to the Wolverine Motor Works and relocated to 12 Huron Street, continuing to manufacture stationary and marine gasoline engines and boats.[5]

In a late nineteenth-century resort brochure published in Holland, the Wolverine Motor Works pointed out that its launches were "handsome, economical, absolutely safe, no government inspection, no licensed engineer, and everybody their own pilot."[6] All of this was possible due to the fact that gasoline launches did not require a licensed engineer to operate the boat because of the lack of a steam engine aboard the boat to power it.[7] In October 1900, company president C.C. Snyder and company secretary

Claude Sintz, the brother of Clark Sintz and also owner of the Sintz Gas Engine Company, announced that the Wolverine Boat Company planned on relocating to Holland in early 1901. Direct access to deeper water meant that it could launch its boats, ever increasing in size and draft. This type of access could not be found in the Grand Rapids area.[8]

By January 1901, the company had signed a long-term lease for lakeside property from J.C. Post of Holland and relocated its boat division from Grand Rapids to Holland.[9] There it worked within a newly built boat factory on the former Anderson Shipyard site, located on the farthest end of West Eighth Street and just east of Washington Avenue. George Edward Clark served as the superintendent of the boat building business for Wolverine Motor Works and oversaw the work of a reported one hundred men.[10] Clark had relocated from Holland to Grand Rapids to serve as designer for the company. Much of the later design work fell to H.J. Perkins, a boat designer from Grand Rapids, or to nationally known marine architect Charles D. Mower.[11]

By January 1901, the company reported that five boats were in production at the new factory, two of which were destined for South America.[12] The trend for larger, lighter, faster launches and ferryboats was keenly seen at the plant, as newspaper reports described the extra

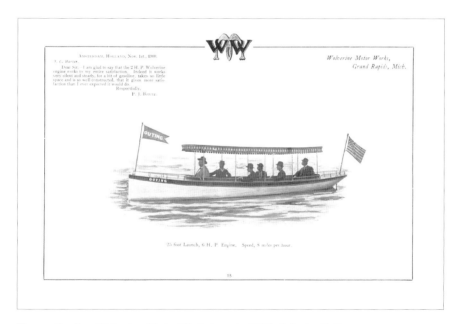

Twenty-five-foot Wolverine Motor Works launch, 1902. *Author's collection.*

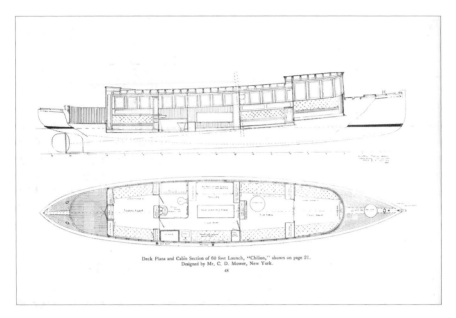

Deck Plans and Cabin Section of 60 foot Launch, "Chilion," shown on page 21.
Designed by Mr. C. D. Mower, New York.
48

Drawings of Wolverine Motor Works launch *Chilion*, 1902. *Author's collection.*

men being hired and the boats being built: a passenger ferry forty feet in length for a customer in Mobile, Alabama; a thirty-five-foot boat for the Baldwin-Ziegler expedition to the North Pole; and a fifty-foot launch for Newberry & Godfrey for a resort near South Haven, Michigan, capable of hauling about two hundred passengers.[13] With the news of more and larger launches being built at the new Holland plant, no mention about the motor division moving was found.[14]

In 1904, the company reported that it was busy building a tug for a Republic of Columbia customer, in addition to building the launches and pleasure boats for other clients.[15] As the motor works plant in Grand Rapids continued to manufacture larger, more powerful engines for its boat customers, it was also looking to move to an even larger plant on the East Coast to make shipping easier and cheaper to its worldwide customer base. By December 1905, it had been reported that the move was inevitable and that six hundred feet of land had been secured on the harbor at Bridgeport, Connecticut, to manufacture motors but that the boat plant would stay in Holland.[16] While the company planned its physical move to the East, it continued to build commercial ferryboats, like the sixty-passenger, forty-eight-foot *Skiddo*, for local customers like the Macatawa Park Company, and a sixty-five-foot pleasure launch powered by a fifty-horsepower Wolverine motor for a customer in Mackinaw City, Michigan.[17]

As the 1905 calendar year drew to a close, and with the fate of the local plant unclear, the company's boat builders continued to make and ship boats, like a forty-foot tug, shipped to Coatzacoalcos, Mexico.[18] In March 1906, news arrived in Grand Rapids and Holland that the company was looking to sell its Grand Rapids and Holland plants and move to Bridgeport.[19] The company continued to produce motorized pleasure boats in Holland until closing the boat making operations and moving the Grand Rapids–based engine plant to Bridgeport in 1907.[20]

HOLLAND LAUNCH AND ENGINE COMPANY

The Holland Launch and Engine Company started in Holland in January 1907 in the former Wolverine Motor Works facility.[21] A subscription drive to raise capital to purchase the former Wolverine Motor Works boat plant had started in early 1906 and was completed by late December with a total $15,000 raised.[22] The officers of the company included Jacob Lokker, president; Herman Garvelink, vice-president and manager; Irving Garvelink, secretary; and Dr. H. Bos, treasurer. The directors of the company included the aforementioned officers as well as John Arendshorst, Benjamin Wolters and Al Klooster.[23] Herman Garvelink, who had produced boats and gasoline engines in Grand Rapids under the Valley City Gas Engine & Launch Company before coming to Holland, brought his machinery to the empty plant and served as the manager at the new company. Garvelink, like

Holland Launch and Engine Company factory, circa 1907. *Lois Jesiek Kayes Collection.*

the investors of the Wolverine Motor Works, was in search of more factory space and shipping facilities like those available on Black Lake.[24]

Garvelink oversaw a crew of ten to thirty craftsmen, depending on demand, as they built launches and gasoline engines for boats and farm purposes.[25] In 1908, Garvelink and Hugh Bradshaw, an investor from Chicago and a Holland summer resident, purchased the company and reopened it after an apparent shutdown.[26] In 1912, the company was shown on local maps on Black Lake between Fourth and Fifth Streets.[27] Little information is known about the company until a 1914 newspaper article reported a lightning strike and a fire at the site causing $6,000 in damages to launches being repaired and built.[28] In 1916, the company appeared on local plat maps at the Fifth Street location but faded from documents after that date.[29]

JESIEK BROTHERS SHIPYARD

The Jesiek family began building boats and running a boat livery in Grand Rapids, Michigan, in 1901. It was situated on the Grand River at the east end of the Wealthy Street Bridge. There they designed, built, sold, serviced and rented boats for all purposes. The Jesiek brothers' boat building company and livery was operated by brothers Gustav, Adolph (Otto) and Joseph Jesiek Jr. The first two brothers had immigrated with their parents, Joseph and Mary, to the United States from Germany in 1882, settling first in Naubinway, a small village on the northern coast of Lake Michigan, in Michigan's Upper Peninsula. By 1893, the growing family had appeared in Grand Rapids, where their father worked as a manager at the Lake Shore House on West Division Street.

In 1900, the Jesiek sons, who now included Rudolph, were working in various furniture factories, like Berkey and Gay; the woodworking skills learned in the furniture trade would no doubt be used a year later to build boats for their fledgling boat building and livery business, which was initially operated at 315 South Market Street, in their spare time. In 1906, Gustav and Joseph Jr. appeared in the local city directory as owning the Jesiek Boat Company at 2–4 Wealthy Street. Brother Rudolph was listed as a boat builder for the firm. By 1908, brother Otto had joined the family business, which now had a thirty-two-page brochure to distribute to potential customers seeking a new boat of their very own, many powered by a new fuel called gasoline.[30]

Jesiek Brothers Livery in Grand Rapids, Michigan, circa 1906. *Lois Jesiek Kayes Collection.*

In 1910, with a $500 loan from brother Rudolph, Joseph Jr. and Otto left Grand Rapids and moved to Jenison Park, west of Holland and located on Black Lake, to form a boat livery, leaving Gus to own the Grand Rapids operation. At this time, Gus moved his company's location to 79–91 Market Street Southwest and enlarged it. His sister, Ann, was his secretary and bookkeeper. Gus continued to make boats of all sizes, many from twenty-five to seventy-five feet in length for customers in Cuba, South America and Australia, until 1920. He would eventually retire to Macatawa, Michigan, to be near his brothers, and passed away there in June 1948.[31]

At Jenison Park, Joseph Jr. and Otto purchased a piece of waterfront land for $175 and took advantage of the growing resort industry on Black Lake by providing ferrying services to tourists arriving on the local interurban line, steam trains and large steamers. They also provided forty clinker-built rowboats through their boat livery, as well as bait and tackle to eager fishermen. They called this company the Jesiek Brothers Livery. In June 1911, they launched the thirty-six-foot *Jenison*, built for the purpose of chartering parties on Black Lake. The *Jenison* was the fourth charter boat they built for use in the charter trade. The others were the *Blitzen*, *Hattie L. V.* and *Pup*. Along with the new boat, the brothers built a new boat landing that year to better serve their customers.[32]

In the fall of 1912, the Jenison Park boat livery facility burned. After the fire, Macatawa businessman Charlie Floyd encouraged the Jesiek brothers to move west to nearby Macatawa to provide service to visiting tourists at Macatawa Park. There, the Jesieks purchased waterfront property, mostly made up of marsh, and built a large building over the water to house their families, in apartments above, with boats and equipment below. At the new location, William "Bill" was born and lived with his parents, Otto and Henrietta (Hattie), and two older brothers, Harold and Donald. Otto and Hattie built a home across the street from the boathouse for their growing family in 1925. Sister Lois was born in that house. Brother Joe Jr. and his wife, Minnie, also built a home that same year next door. The latter home still stands, while the former was razed in 1976.[33]

With the construction of their new building, the newly named Jesiek Brothers Boat Livery continued to promote the rental of its row boats, canoes, large launches and outboard motors; make repairs; and sell bait

Jesiek Brothers Livery crew launching *Jenison*, 1911. *Lois Jesiek Kayes Collection.*

Jesiek Brothers Livery fire, 1912. *Lois Jesiek Kayes Collection.*

New Jesiek Brothers Livery building, 1913. *Lois Jesiek Kayes Collection.*

and tackle to fishermen. The Jesieks also continued to build, rent and place ice shanties for winter ice fishing on Black Lake to promote their business through the colder months, like they had done at the former Jenison Park location.

In 1927, the Jesieks started building small outboard motor–powered hydroplanes called Baby Buzz, as they tried to capture some of the profits associated with building and selling this type of boat. Unfortunately, they did not sell well, and the Jesieks chose instead to sell the Grand Rapids–based Gordon B. Hooton hydroplanes to their customers. That same year, they built their first marine railway to launch and retrieve the ever-increasing number of large power- and sailboats using their anchorages on Black Lake and needing storage during the winter.

In 1928, the brothers officially changed the name of their business to Jesiek's Yacht Basin and Marine Railway in local newspaper advertisements. Invoices used by the company in 1931 called it the Jesiek Brothers Ship Yard and Marine Railway. For sake of brevity, I will refer to the company as the Jesiek Brothers Shipyard from this point forward.[34]

In early 1930, the Jesiek brothers started selling Chris-Craft brand runabouts and launched their largest boat building project to date, the *Patricia*, a thirty-three-foot speedboat designed by its owner, Carl Denkman of nearby Waukazoo and Rock Island, Illinois. One year later, they launched

Launching *Patricia II* at Jesiek Brothers Shipyard, 1931. *Lois Jesiek Kayes Collection.*

Jesiek Brothers Shipyard's International 110 brochure, 1939. *Lois Jesiek Kayes Collection.*

a larger boat for Denkman, called *Patricia II*, a sixty-seven-foot cabin cruiser, in addition to a forty-two-foot schooner sailboat for another customer. In September of that same year, Joseph Jesiek Sr. passed away at son Otto's home in Macatawa Park.[35]

In 1933, Jesiek Brothers recognized the need for a one-design boat for the local racing program to become more orderly and built and marketed a 13.5-foot one-design sailboat called the Crescent. This model of small sailboat sold for $135 completely outfitted and quickly became popular with local and Western Michigan sailors, like those at the Macatawa Bay Yacht Club.[36] The company also built the Charles Raymond Hunt–designed twenty-four-foot International 110 sailboat, which was introduced in 1939, starting with licensed hull no. 300.[37]

Two years later, the Jesieks added a two-hundred-ton marine railway, one of the largest on Lake Michigan. They also moved the former Macatawa Bay Yacht Club building west to their shipyard and used the lower level for offices, while the yacht club used the second floor for meetings. This building was razed in 1976.[38]

Chapter 2

THE GREAT DEPRESSION

During the Great Depression, Holland created an economic organization, the Holland Chamber of Commerce, to enlist corporations to relocate to the area to help provide jobs and economic stimulus to the community. Many types of companies took advantage of the financial incentives offered and moved to Holland, including boat builders.

GIL-BOAT COMPANY

In 1934, the Gil-Boat Company was founded to construct rowboats, unsinkable lifeboats and futuristic cross-lake ferries from rolled steel and aluminum.

The new boat company was formed in June 1934 by Captain Mark L. Gilbert with $10,000 in capital. The factory was located in a portion of the former Ottawa Furniture Company factory at 110 River Avenue, which he leased with an option to purchase.[39] This location gave Gilbert not only ample space to build but also access to Black Lake for launching and testing, as well as consumers passing by on nearby River Avenue. Mark Leroy Gilbert, born in Bristol, Maine, in December 1877, came to Holland from New York City, where he had created a novel, patented manufacturing method for building rowboats and outboard motor–powered boats from arched sheets of 18- to

24-gauge steel—extremely light and rigid boats ranging in length from eleven to fifteen feet.[40]

Financial backers of Gilbert's company included J.J. Shank, Grand Rapids, Michigan; F.E. McFall, president, and J.E. McGowan, treasurer, of a Sparta, Michigan foundry; L.A. Geistert, Grand Rapids; the J.C. Miller Company, Grand Rapids; and George Steketee, John Raven, John Kramer and Walter Steketee, of Holland.[41] In later years, he also constructed custom boats from stainless steel if the customer was willing to pay a little more. While the June 14, 1934 *Holland Evening Sentinel* article sounded promising, it was not until late November 1934 that additional capital from Indiana investors allowed the company to announce that production of boats would finally start in January 1935, with the promise of building 20 to 30 boats per day and employing twenty to twenty-five men.[42] Another article claimed that orders for boats totaled 3,600, 1,400 of which were from southern states, creating a need for a southern boat factory in Miami, Florida. The same article detailed plans to fill an order for a 110-foot oil tanker and 250-foot cruiser for the Russian government and lifeboats for cruise liners. Business looked promising for the young, innovative company.[43]

Up until late 1935, no evidence of Gilbert's steel boats had been documented in any publications other than passing lines from the local newspapers, but that was about to change. In August and September, the periodicals *Iron Age* and *Sheet Metal Worker* published detailed articles about the company that included photographs of the boats and the men building them.[44] Article titles like "Pressed Steel Boats Made without Ribs, Stem or Stern Posts" and "Ribless, Welded Pressed Steel Boats" graced both publications along with detailed, step-by-step photographs and descriptions of the boats first being cut to a pattern and then rolled into a tube and pressed to form breaks that created the keel and chines of the boat. These breaks also created concave curves in the bottom and sides of the boat. Then a bow piece and stern piece were welded to the first piece to form the basic shape, or hull, of the boat. The boat then received seats that were joined to the boat hull using electric and oxy-acetylene welding, to replace ribs normally found in a boat and create air-filled tanks for buoyancy. Once the boat was welded together, a deoxidizing solution was used to treat the steel, followed by a priming coat of aluminum and finished with a coat of long-life paint. The company also made the formed parts of the boat available in kit form that could be shipped, needing only welding to complete the job.[45] The twelve-foot model, the Gil-Row Jr., weighed 116 pounds and could reach speeds of forty miles per hour, with a sixteen-horsepower outboard motor. An undated letter (most likely from 1935) from a customer praised the construction of the Gil-Row Jr. at the Boy's Home Association of Jacksonville, Florida, and promised to spread the word about the company and its boats.[46]

The next year, it became a little clearer as to not only who had invested in Gilbert's company but also their roles in its administration. According to a March 1936 issue of the *Michigan Manufacturer and Financial Record*, officers of the company included Frederick L. Alldis, president; Captain Mark L. Gilbert and Charles S. Huntley, vice-presidents; and John C. Reinke, secretary-treasurer. Directors included Alldis and Gilbert; W.H.

This page: Gil-Boat Company brochure, 1936. *Cherry Overway Collection*.

Kilpatrick, vice-president of Chrysler Motor Parts Corporation; Walter L. Durham, a Detroit capitalist; Senator Edward Brouwer; and Ollie J. Oleson and Byron J. Oades of P.W. Churchman & Company of Detroit.[47] Later that same month, inquiries from a reported ten thousand prospective purchasers and dealers led to a new stock offering of 48,000 of its capital shares to Michigan investors through P.W. Churchman & Company and Whitlock, Smith & Company, Detroit, Michigan. This financing was used mainly for working capital and the purchase of additional machinery and tools. At the time, the firm's capitalization was 250,000 shares of one dollar par value, and they intended to have 125,000 shares outstanding when the offering was completed.[48] The marketing arm of the company, Gil-Boat Sales Corporation, was formed in Detroit during April 1936 with $10,000 in capital, with the intended purpose to buy and sell boats.[49] Employees of the company included Marie de Ridder, stenographer, and Mrs. Elsie Gunn, bookkeeper.[50]

In 1937, Gilbert's company continued manufacturing nine different models of small boats in the Holland plant, ranging in length from eleven to fifteen feet and priced from $32 to $162. In January of that year, the company shipped one hundred metal rowboats in one weekend to the flooded areas of Indiana, which requested five hundred boats for emergency use.[51] In March of that year, G.L. Moorman of Chicago was named president of the company. Other officers' appointments at the time included Edward Brouwer, secretary, and Charles Harrigan, the former plant superintendent, as manager.[52] While the company based in Michigan made and sold smaller boats, Gilbert also continued his plans to manufacture larger boats in other states, like Wisconsin and Georgia, for trade on the Great Lakes, Atlantic Ocean and Gulf of Mexico.[53]

In August 1939, *Popular Mechanics* published a short article, accompanied by photographs of the *Nassau Clipper*, with seven motors turning seven propellers, an unsinkable ship that allegedly skimmed across the surface of the water at a top speed of eighty miles per hour. This 2,150-horsepower, eighty- by twenty-two-foot ship was constructed much like Gilbert's smaller boats, using a concave bottom made of bent steel. The twenty-five-ton boat featured two decks that could accommodate more than two hundred passengers or three hundred tons of freight cargo. Above the waterline, the ship resembled an airplane, using Dow Chemical Company's brand of metal for its construction. The story also mentioned the intention to construct a two-hundred-foot model to be used in the hauling of fruit, vegetables and passengers between Texas,

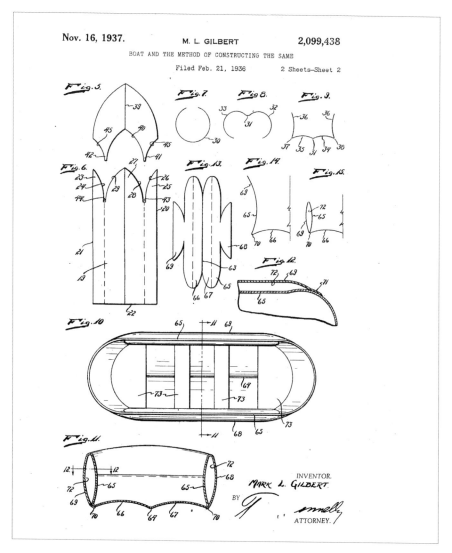

Mark L. Gilbert boat construction patent, 1937. *U.S. Patent Office.*

Florida and New York, as well as allowing aircraft to be launched from its deck without the need for a runway.[54] The story does not mention Gilbert or Gil-Boat Company by name, but the ship is the same mentioned in a July 1939 article in the *Holland City News*. In that article, Gilbert verified that the volplaning boat had been sea-tested in Brunswick, Georgia, and attained a speed of sixty-five miles per hour, with the motors working less than full throttle.[55]

In 1940, the Gil-Boat Company still appeared in the local business directory; however, Gilbert was listed as living in Jacksonville, Florida, and Charles Harrigan was listed as the local contact, serving as secretary, treasurer and manager of the company.[56] In July 1940, the company appeared in a news story as insolvent and owing money to the Jackson-based foundry Potter Manufacturing Company, which had filed suit against Gil-Boat Company in October 1939.[57] The article also detailed that the company was in trouble for failure to file required reports with the state securities commission. No information about the company's fate after that initial court action appeared until the spring of 1941, when local newspapers reported that more claims, other than Potter Manufacturing Company, had been filed in Ottawa Circuit Court, amounting to approximately $40,000. It was also noted that attorney Peter S. Boter had been appointed receiver of the company's assets back in July 1940.[58] One year later, the real estate and personal property of the Gil-Boat Company was sold to local real estate agent John Arendshorst of Holland.[59]

During the turmoil in Ottawa County, Michigan, Gilbert continued working his ideas of building more and larger steel craft for transportation in Florida. In the January 20, 1941 issue of the *Shipping Digest*, an article titled "Something New in Freighters" appeared. Written by Robert J. Gomez of Robert J. Gomez Company, New York, which was listed as an agent of Gil-Boat Company of Florida Inc., the article detailed Gilbert's experimental boat, the Gil-Boat Clipper, earlier referred to as the *Nassau Clipper*, and its 1941 status as charter boat for the Florida-Havana Better Relations Club. In addition to news about the clipper, Gomez detailed Gilbert's plans for two types of cargo freighters: a five-hundred-ton 110-foot version, said to have been started in his Jacksonville shipyard, and a two-thousand-ton version, then preparing to be started. The larger freighters were equipped with derricks to load and unload cargo from the holds of the ship. Their hull construction was much like the *Nassau Clipper*, but with an open deck

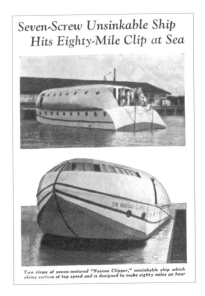

Seven-Screw Unsinkable Ship Hits Eighty-Mile Clip at Sea

Two views of seven-motored "Nassau Clipper," unsinkable ship which skims surface at top speed and is designed to make eighty miles an hour

Nassau Clipper, 1929. *From* Popular Mechanics.

for cargo loading. The estimated speed for both designs was ten to twelve miles per hour.[60] Gilbert himself was also promoting all three types of ships for the war effort to President Franklin D. Roosevelt in January 1942 but could not get an audience with him.[61] It appeared that the lack of financial support and good health had run out for Gilbert and his futuristic ideas. On May 20, 1943, Gilbert passed away in Portland, Maine, at the age of sixty-five from heart failure.[62]

CAMPBELL BOAT COMPANY

In May 1937, Kenneth H. Campbell and his father, Gordon R. Campbell, came to Holland to enjoy Tulip Time. A few months later, the two approached members of the chamber of commerce about locating a new boat building firm in the area to build wooden and steel cabin cruiser boats. At the time, Kenneth's health was progressively deteriorating from Parkinson's disease, and his father, a banker from Calumet, Michigan, wanted to set up a boat company for Kenneth to design boats for and oversee building.[63] Kenneth Hoatson Campbell, born on July 18, 1905, in Laurium, Michigan, received a degree in economics and a certification in business administration from the University of Michigan in February 1926 and a degree in naval architecture at the Massachusetts Institute of Technology (MIT) in 1927.[64] Before leaving to set up his firm in Holland, he was an employee of Luder's Yacht Yards in Stamford, Connecticut; the Elco plant at Bayonne, New Jersey; and the Fore River Ship Yards at Bethlehem Shipbuilding in Quincy, Massachusetts. In 1933, he headed up electric welding specifications for the New York Shipbuilding Company of Camden, New Jersey.[65]

The Campbell boatyard was located at 1691 South Shore Drive in a large three-story building once called the "Beach House," used for housing tourists. When Campbell arrived, it served as the design area and offices for the owner and his crew of boat makers. With Campbell came Iron River, Michigan native Harold Reynolds, a fellow University of Michigan graduate and co-worker at New York Shipbuilding Company.[66] Eldred Sincock, a mine carpenter and neighbor from Calumet, joined the company in 1937 and would eventually become foreman.[67]

In September 1937, Campbell hired local contractor Frank Dyke, builder of the Warm Friend Tavern and Hope Memorial Chapel (now Dimnent Memorial Chapel), to construct a forty- by sixty-foot brick and steel building

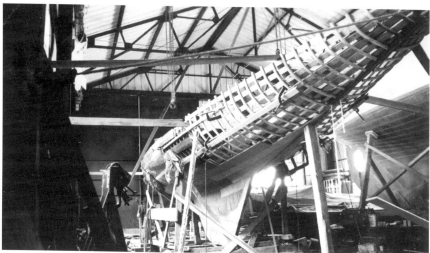

This page, top: Great Lakes 30 design sailboat *Nisswa* under construction, circa 1939. *Campbell Boat Company Collection*.

This page, bottom: 22 Square Meter class sailboat *Pierett* under construction, circa 1940. *Campbell Boat Company Collection*.

Opposite, top: Campbell Boat Company employees at launching of sailboat *Coronado*, 1947. *Campbell Boat Company Collection*.

Opposite, bottom: Campbell Boat Company employees working on boat near docks. *Campbell Boat Company Collection*.

with large glass windows that allowed natural light to illuminate the shop. The building was designed by Peter Elzinga and Harry Colton. Elzinga would go on to cofound construction firm Elzinga and Volkers in 1945 with business partner John Volkers. The new building included a metal shop, boiler room and equipment to heat the large building, as well as tracks built into the concrete shop floor that allowed newly completed and repaired boats, up to fifty feet in length, to be rolled into and out of Lake Macatawa via large boat cradles.[68] An addition to the new building, matching the same dimensions, was constructed in 1939, to provide additional work space for the eighteen-man crew.[69]

Campbell brought with him the knowledge of electrical welding techniques and wooden boat construction. He worked on as many as nine projects at once, including custom-built wooden sailboats like the forty-two-foot *Batavia*, reported as the first Great Lakes 30 design ever built, for J.C. Peterson of Chicago. Other projects included cabin cruisers, scows, pile drivers and fish tugs. Campbell also stored and repaired boats of all sizes and construction types.[70]

In 1940, Campbell changed his advertisements to include custom boat building, now including plywood, and also stock boat designs, like the twenty-six-foot Privateer, a C.B.C. thirty-footer, an eight-foot pram dinghy and the eighteen-foot Charles D. Mower–designed Mower "G," which he had been building since 1938. The company also offered spars, fittings, hauling, storage and repairs.[71] Within a year, the boatyard would be providing military craft to help win World War II.

Chapter 3

THE WAR YEARS

Holland, Michigan, was home to many industries that converted from peacetime manufacturing to supplying the Allies during World War II. Local boat building companies leased space to other companies to build military vessels, while others converted all their production space to build boats that would help win the war.

CHRIS-CRAFT CORPORATION

While most pleasure craft builders in Michigan struggled to survive the Great Depression, the Chris-Craft Corporation of Algonac made plans to expand. And Holland—with its skilled workforce and lack of labor unions—was company owner Christopher Columbus Smith's first choice of location.

In June 1939, the Chris-Craft Corporation, headquartered at 308 Detroit Road, Algonac, Michigan, announced plans to establish a boat building plant in Holland. This plant was the second in what would eventually total sixteen worldwide for the company. Later that year, in August, the Holland Chamber of Commerce specified that the plant would be built on a twenty-two-acre site located on the corner of Douglas Avenue and Aniline Avenue, on Holland's north side.[72] The building of the newest factory in the Holland area got underway on August 2 under the supervision of longtime company employee Arnold William (A.W.) McKerer. He was later replaced by Harry

H. Coll, who then supervised the running of the plant once it was building boats. Like the plant in Algonac, this new factory included a railroad spur connected to the main Pere Marquette rail system in the area. This spur was used to ship raw materials to the plant, which included lumber, chemicals, engines and other boat building supplies, and to ship completed boats to consumers around the country. Work on the 600- by 107-foot plant took place through the summer and fall of 1939 and was written about weekly by local newspapers and monthly by boating magazines.[73] In September, news arrived in Holland that company founder Christopher Columbus Smith had passed away in Algonac at the age of seventy-eight years. Smith had been to the Holland plant site during the planning stages of the expansion.[74] While this must have been a heavy blow to the large and close-knit Smith family, construction continued on the plant, as the company had planned to start building a few models for the 1940 model year by November 15.

In mid-November, construction and plant manager Harry Coll announced that the construction of the plant, the largest boat building plant under one roof for the company, was not completed and set a new deadline of December 1 to start boat production.[75] During the delay, the company provided updates on the progress of the building, which Coll reported was employing up to 70 men. The building was wood framed, covered in galvanized steel and included five hundred windows and five miles of piping for steam heat. The plant was divided into four areas: woodworking mill, hull framing, painting division and final assembly. These areas reflected how a boat was to be built, from raw lumber to finished product. These areas were subdivided into four production lines, much like an automobile plant. The lines included two for the production of low-priced 60-horsepower fifteen-and-a-half-foot runabouts and two for production of 135-horsepower thirty-foot cabin cruisers.[76] In early January, *Motor Boating* magazine announced that production at the Holland Plant had finally begun for the former model, with a projected schedule of two completed boats per day.[77] Following the New York Boat Show in January 1940, reports from the company were positive, as it recorded its best sales at this show since 1929.[78] In early February, the first boat at the Holland plant left on a trailer for the showroom of Spring Lake, Michigan–based Chris-Craft dealer Edward Bauman. The company stated that 108 men were employed at the plant.[79]

In November 1940, *The Rudder* reported that the Chris-Craft Corporation had been awarded a $37,000 contract to build twenty-seven utility speedboats for the United States Army to use for crash boats and rescue boats to retrieve downed aircraft pilots.[80] While these boats were not

Chris-Craft Corporation Holland, Michigan plant, circa 1940. *Author's collection.*

Ed Bauman's Spring Lake, Michigan Chris-Craft boat dealership and marina, 1940. *Author's collection.*

built in the Holland plant, it did signal the company's involvement in the buildup of boats for the military for a possible role in defending American assets against hostile attacks.[81]

In May 1942, after America's entry into World War II, it was announced that the Holland plant, now among three Chris-Craft Corporation plants including Algonac and Cadillac, had been awarded the Navy E burgee (Navy Excellence, later Army-Navy E) for wartime boat production work.[82] This award, presented on June 15, allowed the corporation to not only fly the burgee at the three plants but also use it in any advertising.[83] While it is not clear what models were being built in the Holland plant, it was most likely one of the navy landing boat models.[84] The company was also producing boats for the U.S. Army and Coast Guard. Some of this success can be attributed to key personnel additions, like Gerald VandeVusse, who was appointed personnel manager to refine and expand the human resources program at the plant. VandeVusse's job was made much easier because of the outstanding work ethic of the company's employees and labor force reservoir available in the Holland area, from seasonal farm workers to experienced furniture makers. Coupled with an aversion to unions and strong religious and right-to-work beliefs, it is a wonder that a union was ever formed at the plant. That changed in 1942 when a union organizer from the Higgins Boat Company plant in New Orleans came to Holland to organize the plant. When the vote was taken, 52 percent of the hourly employees voted to unionize, but membership never reached more than 70–80 percent of the workforce, with the balance giving the equivalent of dues to charity. The plant also had a reputation for being a desirable place to work, and existing employees provided new employee referrals, often family members or relatives. There were few dismissals or layoffs, a result of careful employee selection and production planning.[85]

War production continued at a steady pace at the Holland plant on the navy landing craft, which were built during the day and then shipped both by rail and trucks to Algonac for water testing on the St. Clair River.[86] Production on the landing craft was steady until April 1944, when 150 to 270 employees, of a total of 350 at the plant, walked off the job over delays in wage adjustments by the War Labor Board (WLB). Those workers who left were members of four unions in the plant affiliated with the American Federation of Labor (AFL): United Brotherhood of Carpenters and Joiners of America; International Association of Machinists; International Brotherhood of Electrical Workers; and Brotherhood of Painters, Decorators and Paper Hangers of America.[87] A few days later, support

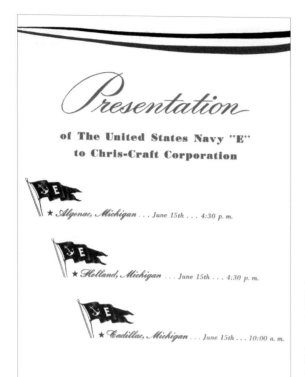

Left: Navy "E" Award program for the Holland, Michigan plant, 1942. *Chris-Craft Corporation Collection*.

Below: Chris-Craft's 8,000th landing craft produced at the Holland plant. *Robert VandeVusse Collection*.

for the walkout extended to the Algonac and Cadillac plants, with a total of 1,000 workers from the three plants.[88] By early May, the WLB agreed to meet with union leaders over the dispute if they returned to work. The unions agreed, the workers returned to work and full production was restored at all three plants.[89] On August 29, 95–98 percent of the plant's workers walked out in sympathy for workers on strike at the Cadillac plant concerning the hiring back of workers after the plant converted back to peacetime production. That walkout ended on October 29.[90]

By the end of the war, the Holland plant had produced more than eight thousand of the twelve thousand landing craft produced by the corporation, many of which were used during the D-Day invasion in June 1944.[91]

Victory Shipbuilding Company

In March 1942, the Victory Shipbuilding Company (also noted as the Victory Shipbuilding Corporation of Holland) leased space from the Jesiek Brothers Shipyard and built two 110-foot wooden submarine chasers to be used by the U.S. Navy to patrol the Atlantic coast for German submarines.[92] One of the reasons Jesiek Brothers might have been chosen was because of the large storage buildings close to the shoreline and the large marine railway that had been built at the shipyard some years before. Even though the largest building available was only one hundred feet long and had a dirt floor, the Jesieks poured a concrete floor and built the ships on an angle within the unheated building until launching the ship via the railway.[93]

The Victory Shipbuilding Company was owned by Illinois residents R.W. Bramberg, chairman, and I.A. Blietz. Bramberg and Blietz hired the Jesiek family to build the boats while they handled the administrative duties, as they readily admitted that they knew little about shipbuilding at a formal welcome given to the men by the Holland Chamber of Commerce in December 1942, one week after the launching of the first ship (USS *SC 1063*).[94] To make up for their lack of knowledge of the boat building craft, the company hired Joe Jesiek Jr. to operate the plant; Kenneth Campbell as naval architect and consultant; Harold Jesiek, in charge of outfitting; Stanley Easter, in charge of engine room; Rex Anderson, production manager; Joe Jesiek, general superintendent; Robert Dawson, civilian inspector; Lieutenant B.J. Platt, naval supervisor; O.W. Lowry, subcontractor; Russell Jesiek, assistant superintendent; Herb Bradley, chief electrician; William Thumm, in charge

Victory Shipbuilding Company–built tug (USS *YT 305*) heading to war, September 1943.
Lois Jesiek Kayes Collection.

of plumbing; Ed Sutton, comptroller; Don Jesiek, in charge of stocks; H.D. Gibson, purchasing agent; and Adrian Klaasen and Paul Seward, diesel engineers.[95] Bramberg and Blietz credited local officials for establishing boat building and blueprint reading classes in the junior high school gymnasium to train local workers for plants such as theirs. More than 130 men were employed at the plant to build the first ship, and an additional 9 guards were employed to patrol the facility and a newly built fence and guard shelters to protect the site from possible sabotage of the two boats, which were the only ones ever built.[96] The second ship (USS *SC 1064*) was launched on January 16, 1943, into an ice-choked Lake Macatawa after being christened by Mrs. R.W. Bramberg.[97] The two boats would later be used alongside each other in active service.[98]

Victory Shipbuilding also built four navy yard tugs. The first (USS *YT 302*) was launched and christened on June 26, 1943, by Mrs. Irving A. Blietz.[99] Each tug took about six months to build. After launching, a few weeks were required to finish fitting out each boat. The last of four tugs to be built and leave the shipyard was the USS *YT 305*, christened and launched by Mrs. Adrian Klaasen on September 11, 1943. It left for active service a short time later.

CAMPBELL BOAT COMPANY

During World War II, the Campbell Boat Company also participated in the war effort by supplying Kenneth Campbell to serve as a naval architect consultant with the Victory Shipbuilding Company at Jesiek Brothers Shipyard. In addition, Campbell's own boatyard provided Osco-Ford conversion marine motor-powered skiffs for the U.S. Army Corps of Engineers and continued filling custom orders for other pleasure craft throughout 1942.[100] But there was still not enough work for most of the crew. In 1943, Eldred Sincock and his family moved to Pontiac, Michigan, to live with his parents and to find work.[101] In 1942, the *Holland Evening Sentinel* announced that Campbell was also a part owner in the Cam-Per Craft Boat Building Corporation. However, this company never built, repaired or rebuilt a boat during its short existence, as far as official records show.[102]

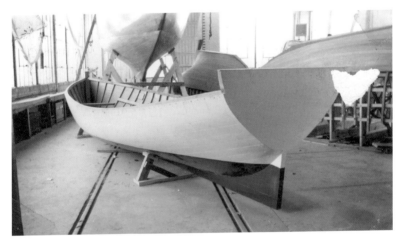

Campbell Boat Company built skiffs for the U.S. Army Corps of Engineers during World War II. *Campbell Boat Company Collection.*

Chapter 4

THE POSTWAR YEARS

The Holland area benefited from the creation of many small boat building firms and the expansion of others in the 1940s and 1950s. New companies sought to fill the need for smaller, affordable wooden boats for consumers returning from war eager to enjoy the freedoms they fought for and spend the money they earned. Other startups saw the chance to introduce new ideas into the boat building industry. Existing companies continued to offer well-crafted traditional wooden planked and plywood sailboats and engine-powered wooden cruisers to wealthy consumers, and others moved away from boat building, sold other manufacturer's boats and made money caring for consumer's boats.

JESIEK BROTHERS SHIPYARD

With the termination of hostilities also came the end of the leasing of the shipyard to Victory Shipbuilding Company and the return of two brothers from the war. After a stint in the navy as a flight instructor, Bill Jesiek returned to Macatawa to join his brothers at the Jesiek Brothers Shipyard. Harold had served in the Coast Guard Reserve and worked as a commercial fisherman and for Victory Shipbuilding Company, along with his brother Donald. While advertisements still listed the shipyard as building boats, it had become obvious that the family was heavily concentrating on selling

Jesiek Brothers Shipyard boat show display, 1949. *Lois Jesiek Kayes Collection.*

Aerial view of Jesiek Brothers Shipyard, 1946. *Lois Jesiek Kayes Collection.*

boats built by companies like Chris-Craft, as well as repairing, maintaining and storing 146 boats of all sizes, selling and repairing Johnson outboard motors; selling paints, varnishes and hardware; adjusting compasses; and providing dockage for approximately fifty boats and haul-out service for boats up to one hundred feet in length.[103] When the company did build boats, they were built custom for local customers wanting the popular one-design racing or sailing classes.

In 1949, Otto Jesiek retired and left the running of the business to his sons Harold, Don and Bill. Otto's business partner and brother, Joe Jesiek Jr., had retired in 1945 and sold his share of the business to Otto.[104] The shipyard was popular with Great Lakes boaters and received quite a write-up in the March 1951 issue of *The Boating Industry*. There, the three brothers—Harold, aged thirty-eight; Don, thirty-seven; and Bill, thirty-two—gave a full account of the direction the shipyard was taking toward marketing its ever-growing marina business, which now included gasoline for customers, a restaurant, showers and restrooms and about sixty-eight thousand square feet of covered storage.[105]

CAMPBELL BOAT COMPANY

After the end of World War II, the Campbell Boat Company picked up right where it left off before the war: servicing, repairing, storing, designing and building custom boats. Many of the employees who had left for other war production jobs in the early 1940s returned, like Eldred Sincock in 1945. Sincock, his wife and their daughter, unable to find living accommodations in Holland, moved into the third floor of the large Campbell house and remained there for eight years. It was one of Sincock's jobs to light the coal furnace that heated the house and boat building plant during colder months each morning.[106] The first boats out of the factory included the twin-engine forty-two-foot sport fisherman cruiser for Ray Kuyper of Holland and a new steel commercial fish tug, *Joann*, for Sewer Brothers of Saugatuck, Michigan.[107] Custom boat building continued throughout 1946 and included a Malabar Jr. sailboat for returning customer W.D. Nansen of St. Louis.[108] That was also the year new employee and University of Michigan graduate in naval architecture and marine engineering Robert Bennett came to work for Campbell. Bennett played a key part in the company by assuming many of the tasks that Campbell could no longer do due to his progressing Parkinson's disease, like handling the naval architecture work, the account books and sales, as well as working in the shop. Mechanic Jim Wetherby joined the Campbell crew the following year. Later additions included mechanics Connie de Young and Harold Reynolds, who also worked on the electrical, welding and engine installation jobs; mechanic and wood craftsman Henry "Hank" Kooker; and the Van Huis brothers, who cut, steam-bent and installed many of the frames and planks on the boats. Bennett left Campbell's in 1949 to work as a naval architect for an East Coast shipbuilding company making boats for the Korean War. He remembered how about six men were always working at the Campbell company while it was active.[109]

In 1947, Kenneth and Mildred Campbell moved to Coronado, California, so that Kenneth could receive treatments for his Parkinson's disease. This was also the second home of one of their favorite customers, Bob Herrmann. The Campbell crew had built Herrmann's forty-two-foot cutter sailboat, *Coronado*, that same year.[110] During the Campbells' absence, the crew, under

Campbell Boat Company–built U.S. Army Corps of Engineers boat, 1946. *Ethel Sincock Collection.*

Campbell Boat Company employees ready a sailboat for launching, late 1940s. *Campbell Boat Company Collection.*

the leadership of manager Reynolds and foreman Sincock, continued to build custom sail- and powerboats made of wood and steel, as well as one-design wooden sailboats like the nineteen-foot Lightning class sailboat, which sold for $1,150, complete with Egyptian cotton sails.[111]

In 1948, the company began building the Campbell-designed twenty-eight-foot Holiday model sailboats. The boat was billed as a fast, sturdy single hander with a roomy cockpit for day sailing and room for two sleeping berths at night.[112] The Lightning class and Holiday sailboats appear to be the company's only stock models of boat built during the late 1940s.[113] In 1950, the crew custom-built another wooden sailboat, a twenty-three-foot Whistler class sloop for Harold L. Parr of Moline, Illinois, to use on Lake Macatawa.[114]

The Campbells returned from California in 1951 to resume the management of the company.[115] That same year, Gordon Campbell, now living back in Calumet, Michigan, funded the Kenneth H. Campbell Foundation for Neurological Research, which is still based in Grand Rapids, for research in organic and functional diseases of the human body.

In the January 1953 issue of *Motor Boating*, the company was listed as building sailboats from nineteen to fifty feet in length of wood and plywood, and by all signs, the company appeared to be in good shape.[116] In June of that same year, Gordon Campbell died.[117] By July, the company property had been leased to the Beacon Boat Company with the option to buy. The crew of six was retained as it completed the 111th boat to be built at the boatyard, which included scows, pile drivers, fishing tugs and sailing yachts. At the time of the leasing, it was reported Campbell had been ill for twenty-three years.[118] Almost a year later, on May 17, 1954, Kenneth Campbell, age forty-eight, succumbed to Parkinson's disease and post-encephalitis, leaving his widow, Mildred, and no children.[119] She passed away in Holland in 1996.[120]

CHRIS-CRAFT CORPORATION

Harry Coll and his wife, circa 1951. *Holland Museum Archives and Research Library.*

As the dust settled from the frenzied war production schedule, the Chris-Craft Corporation was besieged with hourly worker strikes at most of its six plants, which included Algonac, Holland and Cadillac, Michigan; Jamestown, New York; Caruthersville, Missouri; and Chattanooga, Tennessee.

In the spring of 1947, the four hundred workers at the Holland plant began bargaining for increased wages and more time away from the plant. In May 1947, the employees—represented by American Federation of Labor locals for Carpenters and Joiners of America No. 2391; International Association of Machinists No. 1418; Brotherhood of Painters, Decorators and Paper Hangers of America No. 1481; and International Brotherhood of Electrical Workers No. 107—and owners signed a contract increasing wages for all employees by ten cents per hour, one week vacation after one year and two weeks of vacation after four years of employment.[121]

The postwar era for the Holland plant seemed fraught with labor problems, with a hope for a quieter future, but that was not to be. As the company grew in popularity with its pleasure boat line, so did employees' thirst for more money and security in exchange for their hard work.

ROAMER BOAT COMPANY

In 1946, Robert Linn, founder of the Roamer Boat Company, began building and selling cabin cruisers utilizing the special copper alloy steel, which was noncorrosive, and welding the pieces together. The steel plating was 1/8-inch thick for the hull sides and 3/16-inch thick for the bottom, which would give its owners carefree confidence in doubtful waters.[122] Linn took his sales pitch to boat shows around the United States and took on the cabin cruiser competition in this market, which included Safti-Craft, Steelcraft, Higgins and Pacific Boat Building Company, among others.

During the latter part of World War II, Linn oversaw the building of the first Roamer boat, a thirty-foot steel hulled, express cruiser. This boat was built at the Campbell Boat Company site by the Campbell crew, with Linn helping and learning in the process while also selling Steelcraft cruisers as a dealer on the weekends.[123] The boat was designed by Philadelphia-based naval architect J. Murray Watts and featured a mahogany wood cabin.[124] Watts, a designer and builder of steel and iron pleasure boats since 1921, must have been an inspiration to Linn, as he read how a welded steel boat provided owners with a fireproof and leak-proof hull, no seams that moved or needed to be caulked like a traditional wood planked boat, no hull distortion due to the wood bending when not properly stored on a cradle or trailer and no threat from water-based pests like sea worms (teredos). The cost of a welded steel boat was slightly more expensive than a wooden boat under thirty-five feet, but the weight was less because it did not absorb water like a wood boat and maintenance consisted of yearly scraping and painting.[125] By the fall of 1947, Linn and the Campbell crew had finished the boat and called it *Roamer*, which was christened by his wife, Frances, at the Campbell site.[126] That same year, Linn moved to Holland from Grand Rapids with his wife and their two sons, Robert Jr. and David. The young family lived just east of the Campbell Boat Company at 1024 South Shore Drive.[127] The proximity to Campbell's yard made commuting back and forth quite convenient. He leased space from Campbell while a new building was built at 961 Washington Avenue.[128]

In early 1948, Linn moved the company's operation from the Campbell Boat Company plant to his newly built plant. By September of that same year, the factory expanded to include a carpenter shop and an office.[129] His company also appeared regularly in Great Lakes area magazines like *Lakeland Yachting*, where articles and advertisements promoted the beauty and toughness of his boats and used the tagline "They'll Go Anywhere."

Left: Robert Linn, circa 1948. *Roamer Boat Company Collection, Holland Museum Archives and Research Library.*

Below: Roamer Boat Company Washington Avenue plant, circa 1948. *Roamer Boat Collection, Holland Museum Archives and Research Library.*

Roamer Boat Company cruiser under construction, circa 1948. *Roamer Boat Company Collection, Holland Museum Archives and Research Library.*

These advertisements were directed toward forward-thinking consumers who wanted a relatively maintenance-free cruiser over thirty feet that was stylish but also affordable. The advertisements also included news about a passenger boat that could be built for a cost of $4,750 to $6,850 and would seat up to thirty-six passengers, equipped with seats made by Grand Rapids–based American Seating Company. Documented commercial customers of this model included R.B. Zupin Sr. of Elk Rapids, owner of an Elk Rapids–based tour company on Torch Lake, Michigan, and Charter Boat Service of Covington, Kentucky.[130] Linn also worked with the little-known Roland E. Ladewig Company of Grand Rapids, Michigan, to produce a line of thirty-two-foot steel hulled cabin cruisers. Formed in July 1948, the company purchased the boat hulls from Linn and completed interior and cabin tops in a temporary structure next to the Roamer plant.[131]

In 1949, Linn produced a thirty-six-foot line patrol boat for the City of Chicago for use in its drainage canal. He also published his first brochure, which featured a thirty-two-foot cabin cruiser as well as houseboats, fishing boats and work boats. The complete cabin cruisers line, many designed by naval architect A.M. Deering of Chicago, Illinois, included express cruisers, deckhouse cruisers and double cabin cruisers ranging in size from thirty-three to forty-eight feet in length, priced from $9,950 to $15,800. You could even purchase a "handy man's special" model, offered since 1948, that provided you with a hull—and the rest was up to you—at a much lower cost. During the early years, interior finishing was often completed by the buyer even on the stock boats sold as complete.[132] After selling and building one of his large steel hulled boats, Linn launched most of them at Jesiek Brothers Shipyard, where the new owner took delivery. Very few were delivered overland on trailers.

The year 1951 brought big changes to the Roamer Boat Company in its labor force and profit sheet. That July, Roamer announced that it had contracted with the U.S. Navy to produce ten John Alden–designed forty-five-foot steel tugs, powered by diesel engines, worth more than $500,000, to be delivered between December 1951 and June 1952 for use by the Army Transportation Corps. In 1952, a second contract, worth almost $1 million, to build an additional twenty-one tugs was also awarded, forcing the company to devote 85 percent of its productivity capacity to that effort and not cruisers.[133] With it came an expansion to the Washington Avenue plant and a warehouse in Park Township near Lake Macatawa's Big Bayou.[134]

Roamer Boat Company cruiser on Lake Macatawa, circa 1948. *Roamer Boat Company Collection, Holland Museum Archives and Research Library.*

Roamer Boat Company–built tug being launched at Jesiek Brothers Shipyard, 1952. *Lois Jesiek Kayes Collection.*

Ultimately, thirty-one of the tugs were built and 120 persons were involved in the project. The last three tugs headed south in September 1954. Robert Bennett, who served as the civilian inspector for this government contract, remarked in a 2003 interview that that contract got Linn the expertise to go on and build a better cruiser after the war.[135]

With the addition of the warehouse in Park Township in 1954 came plans for Roamer Haven Marina (later Bay Haven Marina) in May 1955.[136] By then, Linn's company had become so successful with the 1955 models, made up of thirty-four- and forty-one-foot lines, and a new dealer network that included St. Louis, Detroit and Chicago that Chris-Craft Corporation had purchased the company in March 1955 for $117,000 and renamed it the Roamer Boat Corporation, a wholly owned subsidiary of the Chris-Craft Corporation. Chris-Craft Corporation owners wanted to enter the welded steel boat business to be competitive with rival metal hulled, inboard motor cruiser manufactures, and Roamer was a natural choice seeing that it was in the same town as one of its largest plants and had proven itself in the marketplace for several years.[137] After selling Roamer to Chris-Craft, Linn and his sons operated Bay Haven Marina at 1862 Ottawa Beach Road in Holland for many years. Robert Linn passed away in 1994.[138]

MAC BAY BOAT COMPANY

The Mac Bay Boat Company was located near the corner of Lake and Fourteenth Streets in the basement of the Bay View Furniture Company and owned by George Arthur Pelgrim; his wife, Eve; and son-in-law, Jim F. White, who had just returned from serving in World War II. Before the war, White had been an avid powerboater, sailor and instructor at the Macatawa Bay Yacht Club. His love of the water, the many hours spent with local boat builder Kenneth Campbell (of Campbell Boat Company) and spending time working in a few areas of Bay View Furniture might have shaped his desire to start a boat building company of his own.[139] Soon, White's father-in-law became involved as an investor, and plans were set for starting a new company. The combination of White's vision and Pelgrim's desire to capitalize on the emerging pleasure boat industry gave birth to the Mac Bay Boat Company.

On May 1, 1948, at 409 West Fourteenth Street, the Mac Bay Boat Company was organized with the following officers: George A. Pelgrim, president and treasurer; Mrs. George (Eve) Pelgrim, vice-president; and Jim White, secretary. The capital stock of the company was valued at fifty thousand shares of the par value of one dollar per share, and starting capital was listed at $10,000.[140] From the beginning, the directors of the new company decided not to use the standard practice of building small runabouts with mahogany planks. Instead, they introduced a sturdy, safe and affordable molded plywood hulled boat equipped with quality hardware and inboard marine motors. This type of hull construction was new to the pleasure boat industry, as it used heat, glue and up to six layers of thin wood veneers molded together to create a sturdy pre-formed hull overnight. Other boat manufacturers, like the Chris-Craft Corporation, were still using planks of expensive Philippine mahogany wood, thousands of screws and days of manual labor. Mac Bay purchased ready-made hulls from several companies—at first from a Canadian company but mainly from United States Molded Shapes in Grand Rapids. The hulls were delivered, sometimes fifteen or twenty at a time, stacked like teacups, via large trailers.

Once the hulls were unloaded, the business of making them into boats was begun in earnest. To turn an unpainted boat hull without a transom into a finished sixteen-foot, 1,500-pound runabout took an engineer and many hours of labor from the company's small group of employees, which numbered twenty. Lester Kaunitz, a Bay City native who first appeared

Looked at from any angle . . .
the **PLAYBOY** *Sportster is*
your *boat for all-round*
pleasure and utility.

15' 10" of speed and class.

72" beam — lots of room.

Genuine Solid Mahogany deck and trim.

Waterproofed one-piece Molded,
U. S. Weldwood Hull.

25—45—75 H.P. Gray Marine Engine.

Speeds up to 40 M.P.H.

In design, engineering, workmanship and finishing, the PLAYBOY has had the
benefit of the best in everything. Low upkeep. Easy portability . . . weighs only
1350 lbs. Trailer, cradle, canvas cover available.

VICTOR E. WATKINS CO.
Office: 5 E. 8th St. — Holland, Michigan
Price subject to change without notice.

Mac Bay Boat Company–built Playboy Sportster brochure, 1948. *Author's collection.*

in Holland in 1947, a longtime boat and travel trailer designer and a man once associated with the Chris-Craft Corporation, was responsible for the design and engineering part of the process.[141] Overseeing the workers was Harry Hopper, production superintendent. Under his direction were craftsmen Alva Burdett (A.B.) Melton (foreman), Donald Van Lare, Gary Versendaal, Doug McKay, Andy Riemersma and William de Boer. After about one week of construction, a glistening white or natural mahogany runabout with a mahogany wood deck would emerge from the basement of the furniture company ready for shipment. Each boat was complete with hardware, a choice of a twenty-five-, forty-five or seventy-five-horsepower Gray Marine engine and seating for five passengers, with a price starting at $1,495.[142]

On June 29, 1948, the first of many Mac Bay Boat Company–built runabouts, sold under both the Mac Bay and Playboy (also seen as Play Boy) names, was sent to a customer in Salt Lake City, Utah. A *Holland City News* article from July 1, 1948, described the new company in detail. According to that front-page article, the Mac Bay–built Playboy Sportster was unique for

Left: Victor E. Watkins, circa 1948. *Author's collection*.

Below: Mac Bay Boat Company plant, 1949. *Author's collection*.

its time since it was the first boat company in the United States to produce an inboard motor-powered (versus an outboard motor) mahogany plywood molded speedboat.

The boats would be marketed to consumers via Holland-based independent boat broker Victor E. Watkins. Watkins was a native of Birmingham, Alabama, said to have come to Holland in about 1937. His daughter, Phyllis Watkins Cox, remembered the family coming to Holland from Muncie, Indiana, where Watkins worked on the Neptune outboard motor for the Muncie Gear Works.[143] From historical sources, such as local newspapers, boating magazines and original sales brochures, it appears that Watkins was working as an independent boat builder and dealer selling Playboy Sportster boats under the Victor E. Watkins Company name in January 1948, a full five months before being hired to sell boats to dealers for Mac Bay Boat Company.[144] While this arrangement eliminated the name recognition gained by having the company name on the boat itself, this was not an uncommon practice, as investors and owners constantly sought to keep payrolls and overhead low through outsourcing.

With Watkins selling the boats under the Playboy nameplate, sales were brisk. According to newspaper sources, trailers loaded with new models left for U.S. distributors as far away as California and international clients in Spain, Portugal, Switzerland, Puerto Rico and Argentina.[145] While the newspapers quoted company officials as producing at least one boat per day with the help of twenty employees, past employees reported that it took more like one week to produce a boat with six to eight employees.

By January 1949, the model name had changed from Playboy to Grayboy and Watkins had added Lester Kaunitz as a partner to his boat brokerage. The change in model names might have been part of Watkins's marketing plan to sell two types of boats: the larger Grayboy runabout and the smaller Playboy Jr. boat powered by an air-cooled Clinton or Wisconsin motor. It is unclear if Mac Bay Boat built the latter.[146] Likely the name Grayboy came from the Gray Marine brand of engine used in the boats.[147] Other than that, only small changes were made to the windshield brackets and deck hardware. Watkins and Kaunitz returned to the New York Boat Show in New York City in January 1949, where spectators were reportedly impressed with America's first molded plywood inboard motor-powered boat, priced at $1,595.[148]

In July 1949, White's wife, Phyllis, was elected as a director for the company during a stockholders meeting. A board of directors meeting was held immediately after, with dramatic changes to the board that included

Mac Bay Boat Company–built Grayboy brochure, 1949. *Author's collection.*

James White being named president, treasurer and manager of the company and Phyllis P. White as secretary.[149] Less than a month later, during a stockholders meeting, the company was sold to A.B. Melton, who then became the sole stockholder. At the same meeting, Melton elected himself as president and treasurer, William E. Burns as vice-president and Dan K. Melton as secretary. It was at this meeting that Melton was awarded a salary of $300 per month and Harry B. Hopper a salary of $200 per month to stay on as the business manager.[150]

Unfortunately, in August of that same year, the sales momentum that Victor Watkins had created tragically ended when Watkins was killed in an automobile accident near Elmira, Michigan. Kaunitz, the driver of the automobile, survived with bruises and broken ribs.[151] According to newspaper reports, Watkins and Kaunitz were on their way to Petoskey with a Grayboy runabout in tow when Kaunitz was blinded by the headlights of an oncoming automobile and lost control of the car. Their vehicle hit a utility pole, throwing Watkins from the car. Watkins, aged fifty-eight, died early the next morning in a Petoskey hospital, hours before they were to have demonstrated the boat for a potential customer.[152]

After Watkins's death, sales dipped dramatically, according to sources associated with the company. Soon after this tragedy, Kaunitz left Holland and the company. He continued in the boating industry as a designer, appearing in Bay City in 1952 and Lake Providence, Louisiana, in 1958 at the new factory site for the Little Rock, Arkansas–based Bowman Manufacturers Inc.[153] He passed away while living in Grosse Pointe Park, Michigan, in 1976.[154] William de Boer, who started at the Mac Bay company in 1948, remembered that soon after Watkins's death, the employees were given a "vacation"—or they could take out their back pay in tools, which he opted to do.[155] William de Boer and two other employees, Andy Riemersma and his brother, stayed with the company, even as the company appeared to be finished.

By November 1952, the company had moved to new quarters at 9 West Seventh Street in preparation for the sale of the Bay View Furniture factory to neighboring business H.J. Heinz Company.[156] At the new location, the company expanded its offerings to the public with the introduction of the twenty-foot Express model cabin cruiser, which could be powered by an outboard or inboard motor; an open utility model using the same hull as the

Mac Bay Boat Company Seventh Street plant. *Mac Bay Boat Company Collection.*

cruiser without the cabin top, in addition to the original inboard runabout model, now missing the Grayboy moniker; and smaller outboard-powered models in twelve- and fourteen-foot lengths.[157] William de Boer remembered making about twelve cruisers before Melton sold the business to George Dobben of North Muskegon on December 20, 1954, for $9,832.34, receiving all ten thousand shares.[158]

The Dobben family had been interested in buying the company outright since its days at Bay View Furniture and had been loaning money to the pair since relocating the company to 9 East Seventh Street. Shareholders included George J. Dobben; his son, Clifford G. Dobben; Clifford's wife, Jo Ann M. Dobben; George P. Ballas; Peter G. Ballas; Douglas and Mary Maples; Fred Eller; and Barbara Dobben.[159] Many of the same shareholders also became the new board of directors, with George Dobben serving as president, Clifford Dobben G. as vice-president, George Ballas as secretary, Fred Eller as treasurer and Douglas Maples as director.[160] Under new ownership, the company again flourished, still using United States Molded Shapes Inc.–built hulls for its line, which now included the outboard-powered thirteen- to nineteen-foot models, as well as a twenty-one-foot inboard-powered model.[161] The company remained at the East Seventh Street location for a short time before relocating to a plant four times the size of the old location two miles north of Holland on what was described as "the Lake Road."[162] It then relocated to a new factory at 5605 Airline Road in Muskegon Heights in May 1956.[163] Officials closed down the company in 1964.[164]

Chapter 5

THE FIBERGLASS '50s

During the 1950s, local boat builders experimented with new materials developed during the war effort, especially fiberglass. Fiberglas was created by the Owens-Corning Fiberglas Corporation of Toledo, Ohio, in 1938 and was initially used as insulation for homes and businesses. Combining fiberglass and polyester resins (Fiberglass Reinforced Plastic, or FRP) to build a boat first came about in 1942 with the groundbreaking work of Ray Greene of Ohio.[165] Although established companies found it hard to abandon traditional wooden boat craftsmanship for "plastic," the affordability and reduced maintenance of fiberglass boats made them popular with the public. Little did they know that this would allow boat design changes that would lead to new boat sales and increased profits. This technology steadily spread throughout American boat manufacturing plants, including Holland, Michigan, placing that town among the leaders in the industry.[166] A few independent visionaries worked to perfect their production, while others did not.[167]

JESIEK BROTHERS SHIPYARD

By 1954, the United States had an estimated 2 million people enjoying close to 500,000 boats. One-fifth of those boaters used the Great Lakes to find relaxation, and some of those boaters used the Jesiek Brothers

Shipyard, thought to be the biggest shipyard on Lake Michigan at the time, for service and docking.

In August 1956, Joe Jr. passed away at age seventy-three, leaving Otto as the lone surviving son of the original Jesiek brothers. In addition to his widow, Joe's son, Russell J., survived him and continued to work at the shipyard.[168] That same year, the shipyard started building boats again, like the International 110 class sloop sailboat. The Macatawa Bay Yacht Club had hosted eight boats in this class in 1947, but the boats had come from other licensed builders, like Lawley and Campbell Boat Company, just down the lake. In the early 1950s, Bill Jesiek purchased and raced a 110 through the club, along with many other local sailors. With permission from the International 110 Association, the shipyard returned to building and selling the 110s in 1956 as clubs around Michigan, like those at Gull Lake and Bay City, formed and populated their fleets with these boats. Jesiek started heavily advertising to potential 110 owners in popular Great Lakes–area boating magazines starting in 1957 and ending in June 1959. Jesiek is cited as one of the two principal builders of this class, along with Graves Yacht Yard Inc. of Marblehead, Massachusetts.[169]

Tragedy struck the Jesiek family twice in August 1958 when Otto's oldest son, Harold, passed away in a drowning accident off of Saugatuck at age forty-six.[170] Otto's wife, Henrietta, passed away later that same month.

Jesiek Brothers Shipyard employees, circa 1940s. *Lois Jesiek Kayes Collection.*

Jesiek Brothers Shipyard–built International 110, 1950s. *Lois Jesiek Kayes Collection.*

Surviving sons Bill and Don purchased their late brother's ownership in the shipyard from Harold's widow, Lenore.

With the passing of a brother and mother also came the end of boat building at Jesiek Brothers Shipyard on any large scale, choosing instead to sell boats manufactured by large manufacturers, mentioned earlier, as well as smaller sailboat builders like Ferrier Marine's Silhouette Mark II, O'Day fiberglass sloop sailboats and Phil Rhodes–designed and Palmer Johnson–built 40 Rhodes Cutter sailboats.[171] With this model, the shipyard continued on a track to become one of the largest and most successful marina and shipyards on the Great Lakes.

In June 1973, Jesiek brothers Bill and Don sold the shipyard to Herb and Roger Eldean, who then formed the Eldean Shipyard.[172] Don Jesiek passed away from cancer in April 1995, and Bill Jesiek passed away on August 13, 2012, in Holland at the age of ninety-three.[173]

CHRIS-CRAFT CORPORATION

In July 1950, the Chris-Craft Corporation announced plans to add a $100,000 88- by 600-foot addition to the east side of the existing plant. When it was completed in November of that year, the new addition brought the overall square footage of the plant to more than 117,000 square feet, adding two hundred more jobs to the plant's already four-hundred-member-strong labor force.[174] The work was completed by Owen Ames Kimball Company of Grand Rapids, Michigan, and utilized many local construction laborers to build the steel frame and cement block addition. The addition added three assembling lines to the existing six and increased the production of the plant by 50 percent, according to plant manager Harry Coll. This increase in space and craftsmen also allowed the plant to build larger cruiser-type boats up to fifty feet in length, instead of being restricted to thirty-four feet as before.[175]

By the early 1950s, the Holland plant was one of three producing the cruiser lines along with Algonac (large) and Chattanooga (small). The smaller runabout line was produced at the Cadillac plant, while Holland produced the medium-size line of cruisers, ranging in size from thirty-one to thirty-eight feet, and because of a skilled workforce and recent plant expansions, it could also build the larger and smaller lines when demand warranted it.[176]

Labor negotiations resumed in 1953 following the end of the Korean War and wage stabilization policies, ending in the signing of a new contract in March.[177] The new contract, negotiated between the representatives of the corporation and the American Federation of Labor locals for Carpenters and Joiners of America No. 2391; International Association of Machinists No. 1418; and Brotherhood of Painters, Decorators and Paper Hangers of America No. 1481 included a $40 Christmas bonus for all employees and an increase in hourly wages between $0.07 and $0.17 per hour for the top five skilled classifications.[178] In May of that year, corporation representatives announced plans to expand the plant's footprint with a 200-foot addition to the south end of the building, which at the time measured 200,000 square feet. Some sources peg the addition at 240 feet. This announcement also included a prediction that the increased size of the plant would also increase the size of the labor force by 25 percent to the already 550 employees. The expansion of the plant was completed in 1954 and included a car wash–style unit for testing cruiser cabins and superstructures for leaks.

Labor negotiations continued in January 1954 but broke down on March 17 as employees formed a picket line outside the plant. The majority of the

Aerial view of the Chris-Craft Corporation Holland plant, July 6, 1956. *Roger MacLeod Collection, Holland Museum Archives and Research Library.*

Holland plant employees joined the hourly employees of the Algonac and Cadillac plants. Employees from the three plants bargained for increases in wages, additional insurance benefits and additional vacation time for longtime employees. One week after the beginning of the strike, violence erupted outside the plant as local employee picketers were joined by those from the Algonac plant. The violence included smashing car windows of workers driving through the picket line and attempts at turning at least one car completely over with the driver still in it. That same day, plant manager Harry Coll, citing the violence as the main cause, closed the plant and stopped work on fire prevention measures. Production had stopped sometime earlier.[179]

On March 26, representatives from the three Michigan plants met with corporation representatives to hammer out a solution to the dispute between the nearly two thousand striking Michigan employees and the boat corporation representatives. While Holland plant manager Coll and assistant plant manager Russell Fredericks were not present, local union representatives were, including plant employees Ray Wallick, who served as bargaining committee chairman; Peter Van Iwaarden; Neil Diekema; and Jacob Witteveen. The plant remained open to management and secretarial employees, while the factory gates were manned by a small force of hourly employee picketers.[180] On April 8, assistant plant manager Fredericks announced that fourteen office employees had been laid off, while specifying that the negotiations in Detroit concerned only the Algonac plant and not the Holland plant.[181] That same day, as corporation representatives in Detroit pushed for separate plant negotiations, Fredericks wired a telegram to the presidents of the three unions that read, "Lack of orders and the continuing business recession make it advisable for the corporation to withdraw all wage increase and fringe benefit offers, and notice is hereby given to that effect. We further suggest that all employees with low seniority seek employment elsewhere." Cadillac plant manager Frank Kelly issued the same statement to his striking employees.[182] A little over a month after the strike had begun, it ended with the individual plants negotiating and receiving different deals. The 767 hourly rated Holland plant employees received a five-cent-per-hour increase plus six paid holidays, a modified union shop with check-off system, top seniority for committeemen and a Christmas bonus. The new contract was scheduled to last until March 1, 1955.[183]

On Monday evening at 10:29 p.m., May 23, 1955, the thirty-five- by ninety-six-foot office area of the boat plant, which was added to the plant in 1943, caught fire after a lightning strike to the roof during a strong electrical storm. While the main plant was a mere twenty feet away, it did not catch fire during the four-hour battle with the blaze. The estimated seven hundred workers working at the plant on the daytime shift were gone, but a small crew was on hand during the evening and started fighting the blaze soon after it was discovered and continued when local fire departments arrived on the scene.[184] A new office area was later added to the southeast corner of the plant.

Earlier that year, in March 1955, the Chris-Craft Corporation purchased the locally owned Roamer Boat Company, and Harry Coll was named president of the Roamer Boat Corporation and corporate vice-president of the Holland Division, which included the Roamer plant and the wood boat plant. With him came George Smith as chief engineer. Russ Fredericks was appointed plant manager of the wood boat plant to replace Coll. Later in the decade, the Holland plant continued to show its flexibility in boat construction by working with the other plants to build boats in demand by

Left: Roamer Boat Corporation advertisement, July 1955. *Richard Sligh Collection*.

Right: Parsons Corporation employees testing a Lake 'n Sea fifteen-foot Pleasure Runabout, 1958. *Lee Wangstad Collection*.

consumers, like the plywood Cavalier line, with the Chattanooga, Tennessee and Salisbury, Maryland plants.[185]

Chris-Craft took notice of small upstarts like the Slick Craft Boat Company, using the new fiberglass construction method, but labeled it a fad and continued using wood to build its new designs. For a few years, this approach worked, but as the demand from boat-hungry, postwar consumers grew, it could no longer ignore the very real threat fiberglass boat building pioneers posed.[186]

In 1955, fiberglass boat construction technology came to the state's largest boat manufacturer with the news that Chris-Craft was using a large gold fiberglass fin and engine cover on the afterdeck of its new eighteen- and twenty-one-foot Cobra models. It is unmistakable that this changed the styling trends for the company moving forward, as it sought to retain its global base of consumers, whose tastes were changing. It also signaled that the company was ready to add fiberglass components to its boats, like cabin tops to its cruisers and fins to its runabout line. The company sought to expand its footprint in the market in the summer of 1957 when it purchased the Lake-N-

Sea brand of boats from Lakensea Boat Corporation, a division of Southern Plastic Corporation based in Boca Raton, Florida.[187] Correspondence from Vice-President Wayne Pickell outlined the new purchase:

> *Spiraling sales of practical and stylish outboard motors by many manufacturers has created a broad new market for low-cost outboard boats. Lake-N-Sea Boats will develop a line of durable fiberglass boats that reflect both unique styling made possible by molded fiberglass construction and low prices resulting from volume production.*[188]

While the division lasted only one year, it did reflect how much the company needed to learn about working with fiberglass technology before trying again. While the company pondered its transition to the use of fiberglass and resin to build entire boats, the company finished the last year of the decade grossing $40 million, with earnings of $2.5 million building wood boats.[189]

ROAMER BOATS CORPORATION DIVISION OF CHRIS-CRAFT CORPORATION

In March 1955, the Chris-Craft Corporation announced plans to get into the steel boat building industry with the purchase of the locally owned Roamer Boat Company assets and trademark, creating a wholly owned subsidiary, the Roamer Boat Corporation. Harry Coll was named president of the new corporation and corporate vice-president of the Holland Division, which included the local wood boat plant. Chris-Craft expanded the original 961 Washington Avenue plant to nearly twenty thousand square feet soon after the purchase and introduced subtle design changes to the Roamer line.[190] By May 1955, advertisements under the new name appeared in popular boating magazines with a dramatic flair that had not been seen under the Robert Linn ownership. The only length and model offered was the thirty-five-foot express cruiser. The styling and options made in the 1956 line kept the thirty-five-foot length and expanded the deck options to four different types.[191]

In May 1956, the subsidiary announced that it had purchased a forty-five-acre tract to construct a new eight-hundred-foot-long factory, located at 222 Lakewood Boulevard, to produce pleasure, commercial and military

Roamer Boat Corporation brochure, 1957. *Roamer Yachts Division of Chris-Craft Corporation Collection.*

Roamer Yachts plant, 1962. *Author's collection.*

models ranging in size from 25 to 45 feet, under the leadership of newly appointed plant manager Michael Potter. Potter had joined Robert Linn at the Roamer Boat Company in 1950 and stayed with Roamer after the sale to Chris-Craft.[192] Sales manager Ken Tysee predicted that up to four hundred employees would be needed at the 170,000-square-foot plant. The plant, referred to as the Roamer Steel Boats Division of Chris-Craft Corporation, opened for production in 1957 with departmentalized lines on various floors that fed into the six main floor assembly lines for installation running the length of the building.[193]

In late 1958, Harry Coll was promoted to president of the Chris-Craft Corporation and moved to the new headquarters in Pompano Beach after twenty years at the Holland plants. It is unclear who replaced him as vice-president of the Holland Division until Russell Fredericks was appointed in 1960.[194] The decade ended with the company building twelve different steel boat models ranging in size from twenty-eight to fifty-two feet.[195]

BEACON BOAT COMPANY

The Beacon Boat Company, headed by Orville Alf Munkwitz, leased the Campbell Boat Company yard from Mildred Campbell starting in July 1953. Munkwitz was born on July 14, 1910, in Swan River, Manitoba, Canada, and later attended Bay View High School in Milwaukee, Wisconsin, where he studied manual arts. After graduating high school in 1928, he studied architecture at the University of Michigan. Upon graduation, he worked at American Shipbuilding Company, American Bureau of Shipping and Manitowoc Shipbuilding Company before leasing the Campbell plant.[196]

By 1954, the Beacon Boat Company was constructing and selling boats built of wood or steel for sailing and powerboating. Examples included kits, semi-built or fully built wooden nineteen-foot Lightning class sailboats and a thirty-one-foot, twin-engine welded plate steel Sport Cruiser model for domestic consumers, as well as wood minesweepers and twenty-six forty-foot wooden hulled utility boats for the U.S. Navy to use for the Korean War.[197] The first of the utility boats (C-124436), built using double planking of Alaska cedar inner layer and Philippine mahogany outer, was launched at the boatyard on December 6, 1954, with Mildred Campbell doing the honors, and shipped to Philadelphia via truck later that same month. Beacon was the first boat building company of many

Beacon Boat Company employees launching a forty-foot U.S. Navy utility boat, circa 1956. *Joint Archives of Holland Photograph File.*

other companies to complete the first hull for the navy contract.[198] By March, it had completed the sixth hull for the contract and was receiving and using the navy official's praise for high quality and delivery time in its advertising.[199] Many of the 17,550-pound, seventy-five-man-capacity utility boats were used aboard ships like the newly built USS *Forrestal* (*CV-59*), the first supercarrier in U.S. Navy history.[200] Military and domestic contracts forced the company to expand beyond its ten-man crew, but no details were found. Known employees included Fred Holthuis, Albert Kortman, William Staal, Chester Kuipers, Dick Langermaat and Harold Reynolds. Longtime employee and foreman Eldred Sincock and Munkwitz found it hard to work together, so Sincock moved out of the third floor of the company house, after ten years of calling it his home, and left to work for the local Chris-Craft Corporation plant and eventually the Roamer Steel Boat Division of that corporation.[201]

The navy contract was still in place when the company announced in late 1955 that it would be building and selling the C. Raymond Hunt–designed twenty-nine-foot, ten-inch International 210 sailboat for $2,400 without sails, the Sparkman & Stephens–designed thirteen-foot, six-inch Blue Jay for $770 without sails and the Lightning sailboat offered before the contract, for $1,750, with sails.[202] Clearly, it was preparing for a return to more pleasure boat building.

In March 1956, with the navy contract complete, Beacon turned all its energy to building many types of stock wooden sailboats and steel powerboats, as well as custom sailing yachts. Munkwitz even invited consumers to make a visit to the boat building plant to inspect the crew's work through local newspapers and national boating magazines.[203] The plywood-constructed International 110 sailboat was offered by the company starting in March 1957 in addition to the larger International 210, Lightning and Blue Jay.[204] In December 1958, the company announced an order for seven more International 210 boats to be delivered to fleet owners in Muskegon for the 1959 sailing season, totaling eleven for that area, and one for the 1958 International 210 national champion, Richard Sullivan of Boston, for sailing in the Cohasset, Massachusetts fleet.[205] In 1959, the company offered a newly designed Alvin Mason thirty-two-foot steel cruiser for sale to consumers for $2,000, the fifteen-and-a-half-foot William Crosby–designed Snipe sloop and Inland Scow sailboats, but little was written about these new models.[206]

In May 1959, *Lakeland Boating* magazine announced that Orville Munkwitz had formally purchased the Campbell Boat Company property from the Kenneth H. Campbell estate, which he had been leasing since 1953. In the story, Munkwitz said that he wanted to concentrate on building only yachts and small commercial craft, as well as servicing boats of all types, with no mention of the many sailboats they had been building and selling. Sometime between 1960 and 1962, Beacon closed its doors.[207] Little is known about Munkwitz after leaving Holland, except that he passed away in Portland, Oregon, on September 25, 1985.[208]

SKIPPER-CRAFT BOATS

Skipper-Craft Boats was founded by Jason Petroelje, the son of a Zeeland, Michigan carpenter. Petroelje grew up around wood and enjoyed the things you could do with it. In 1949, the young but already skilled Petroelje landed a job at the local Chris-Craft plant. There he learned the art of building fine wood cruisers and the value placed on them by consumers. Petroelje took this knowledge home, and with scrap lumber purchased from Chris-Craft, he built a mahogany plank outboard motor–powered boat based on plans he found in *Mechanics Illustrated* magazine. For ten months, the project consumed his spare time. "My dad had a pretty good-sized chicken coop there, and he wasn't using it anymore. So I built four boats in that chicken coop over a period of about three years, improving on them and making a nicer boat and better performing boat each successive time," he recalled in a 2000 interview. After those magazine-inspired boat projects, Petroelje began designing his own outboard boats and constructing them from marine-grade sheet plywood, a product used heavily by boat manufacturers during World War II. No longer did you have to have thousands of dollars and a boathouse to own a motorboat. After purchasing a Skipper-Craft for about $2,000, a trailer and outboard motor, Petroelje's customers were free to enjoy them anytime on any body of water they chose. Freedom like this spurred a huge postwar boating craze throughout the United States that has continued to this day.[209]

Petroelje continued to make boats in his spare time until 1952, when he left Chris-Craft due to a labor strike and a desire to create his own fine boats. His new company, Skipper-Craft Boats, was made up of himself and a few helpers, like Warren Thompson, Gene Gort, Jacob Steenwyk, "Pug" Yonker and Dick Schutt. The new company was located at 249 East Twenty-Sixth Street in Holland, where the company built stock and custom fourteen- to eighteen-foot sheet plywood outboard boats with plywood mahogany decks. Each boat took about eighty hours to build and included fine craftsmanship and quality materials that continue to serve many Skipper-Craft collectors on the water.[210]

The company produced its first brochure in 1957, which included four models in any color scheme the customer wanted. Models included the sixteen-foot Panther, Custom Runabout, Sportsman and eighteen-foot Voyager. Six eighteen-foot molded mahogany inboard Panther models were built after local Hollander Willis de Boer asked Petroelje to build an inboard Skipper-Craft boat with the name "Panther" on the transom. These rare models sold for $6,000 each. After De Boer's contract was completed, Petroelje created a sheet plywood Panther model, complete with two separate cockpits and a small mid-deck. These early models were painted black and decked with mahogany plywood, which included a blonde king plank and covering boards, as well as upholstery on the interior sides and seats. Later models were designed without the mid-deck and included automobile industry–inspired fins and two-tone appearance, with a chrome or polished

Skipper-Craft Boats display at a Grand Rapids boat show, circa 1956. *Author's collection.*

aluminum strip dividing the colors. Two-tone color schemes included white and natural mahogany. By 1959, automotive industry–inspired fins were nicely integrated into the sides of the boat, whereas earlier models' fins appeared to be an afterthought.[211]

Skipper-Craft Boats sold most of its inventory to Western Michigan customers through boat shows, visits to the boat shop and word of mouth. A Detroit, Michigan dealer sold a few boats, but many were sold by Petroelje right in Holland. In 1959, boating consumers' desire for cheaper and lower-maintenance fiberglass boats forced Petroelje to close the company and work for another boat building firm in Holland, under the direction of boating industry legend George Glenn Eddy. This venture, called Powerboats Inc., was short-lived for Petroelje, who acted as foreman of a dozen men on the construction of thirteen twenty-two-foot sheet plywood outboard motor–powered boats. The company lasted about one year before the doors closed. Afterward, Petroelje became a carpenter for a Holland-based construction firm Elzinga and Volkers before retiring.[212] He passed away on April 25, 2015.[213]

POLL MANUFACTURING COMPANY

The history of building fiberglass boats in Holland, Michigan, began with a young Clyde Poll. In 1954, a year after graduating from Holland High School, he started Poll Manufacturing Company with his father and built the Wonder Craft line of boats at 351 East Sixth Street, right next to his father's residence.[214] "I liked boats and I thought, well, I'll fool around and try and build some fiberglass boats. So I did that. Wood was on the way out anyway," said Poll in a 2001 interview.[215] Poll started out by having two molds built, one fourteen feet and the other sixteen feet, mounted on steel framework that allowed the workers to rotate the mold to the desired angle for working within the mold. The plug and mold were made by Skipper-Craft Boats owner Jason Petroelje.

The workers—including Harry Laarman, Keith Wilterdink and Poll's father-in-law, Herman Jager—built the fiberglass boat by first applying a releasing agent, like paste wax, to the inside surface of the mold and then polishing it smooth. The wax allowed the finished boat to be removed from the mold without harming the exterior surface of the boat hull. Next, the workers sprayed a coat of resin referred to as the gel coat and then added a layer of fiberglass cloth to form the outside surface of the boat. Additional coats of resin without tint and fiberglass matte were added, one after another, finishing with a layer of fiberglass roving until the hull was thick enough to maintain its integrity. After the last coat of resin cured, workers lifted the boat hull from the mold. Poll's crew painted the boat once it was removed from the mold. Once the hull was out of the mold, workers added structural support to the inside of the hull using locally milled white pine or imported mahogany. The support consisted of two stringers and a keel that ran the length of the boat and a plywood transom to cap off the stern. These pieces were fastened to the boat hull using a layer of fiberglass roving and resin.[216]

Once that was done, either a wooden deck of plywood, plank wood or fiberglass was attached to the hull. Very few wooden decks were ever built due to maintenance and consumers' desire for an all-fiberglass boat. Once the deck was placed on the hull, much like a shoebox lid and box in the case of a fiberglass deck, it was attached with screws and a bead of sealer between the two to prevent leaking. The crew installed a plywood floor; plywood bench seats; a steering wheel attached to a cable and pulleys that attached to the outboard motor; windshield; deck hardware like lights, cleats and rope chocks; and trim around the outside of the deck.

A restored 1957 Wonder Craft boat, 2010. *Darrin Podskalny Collection.*

Most of the hardware used on Poll's boats came from Grand Rapids–based Attwood Brass Works. The wooden components came from Harry Hamburg's Holland-based lumber mill or importers. The seat upholstery was provided by Warren Veurink in color schemes that went with the boat and were chosen by the customer. Many were black and white, with some red and white. After the boats were completed, Poll's crew would mount an Evinrude, Johnson or Oliver twenty-five- or thirty-five-horsepower outboard motor to the boat, depending on the size and brand desired by the customer.[217]

In December 1955, Leon Slikkers, owner of the newly formed Slick Craft Boat Company, contracted with Poll to build fifty fiberglass hulls for Slikkers's boat company's 1956 model line, to which Slikkers then added mahogany plywood decks and seats. This contract was completed later that year. Poll continued making Wonder Craft brand boats and selling plain hulls to other boat builders, like Lubbers Marine & Sport Center in Hudsonville and Ken Cook, maker of Ken-Craft boats in Holland, through the late 1950s. Poll even sold complete boats equipped with trailers and Elgin brand outboard motors to the local Sears store as Elgin branded boats, which was owned by Sears and Roebuck Company, but this arrangement proved to be too much hassle for Poll.[218]

In 1960, Poll closed the company for many reasons, some of which included having no real marketing plan other than word of mouth of customers, local boat shows and advertising in the *Holland Sentinel*; Slick Craft Boat Company starting making its own fiberglass boats; Lubbers and Ken Cook being unable to sell enough of their branded boats for Poll to make any money as a supplier of hulls; and Poll having grown tired of working with fiberglass and resin (his constantly changing workforce felt the same way). According to Poll, the company made between three hundred and four hundred boats, including those hulls made for other companies, between 1954 and 1960.[219]

SLICK CRAFT BOAT COMPANY

Leon Slikkers registered the Slick Craft Boat Company name in June 1954 and offered production models in 1955. His goal was to build quality boats that were also affordable to consumers.[220]

In 1946, eighteen-year-old Leon R. Slikkers, the eighth of nine children, left his family farm in Diamond Springs, Michigan, and began building boats at the local Chris-Craft plant. His desire to avoid a career in farming made his decision to join his brothers Gerald and Dennis at one of Holland's largest factories an easy one.[221] In a 2002 interview, Slikkers explained, "I love working with my hands, and making and creating. So when I got a job at Chris-Craft, I really fell in love with it, because it was making things out of wood, which I like best of all."[222]

Once Slikkers landed a position at Chris-Craft, he was assigned to the joiner department to make cabin tops. As the months went by, he quickly learned and refined his craft with the help of mentors like his first foreman, Herm Volkers, and fellow employee Harry Busscher. "[Harry Busscher] taught me an awful lot....[H]e just was careful of helping me to select the right tools, how to sharpen my tools, how to do the job proficiently with good quality. He was a good craftsman." Slikkers learned quickly from his mentors, and by the time he reached age twenty-four, he had been promoted to assistant foreman of the joiner department. Some of Slikkers's fellow workers, such as Merle Cook, had noticed his abilities; Slikkers had an uncanny ability to create new designs. "Whenever they engineered a new boat, he was instrumental in a lot of the changes— carrying out and building the mock-ups and cutting the patterns—because he was really skilled," said Cook in a 2002 interview.[223] Slikkers continued his successful career at Chris-Craft and thought little of changing jobs until he experienced labor strikes.

In 1952, during a company-wide labor strike, Slikkers and fellow Chris-Craft employee Jason Petroelje decided to build their own boats. During the strike, Slikkers and Petroelje produced approximately ten runabouts made of sheet plywood, averaging fifteen feet in length. These unbranded outboard motor–powered boats had painted hulls and varnished mahogany decks and were sold out of Slikkers's garage. After the strike ended, the two men decided to end the partnership; Petroelje wanted to leave Chris-Craft to build boats full time under the Skipper-Craft name, and Slikkers wanted the security of a paycheck from Chris-Craft. Slikkers recalled, "I still kept building some boats from the design we had, and I would sell them and work on the weekends. I started to build contacts and kind of knew of what the industry would be."[224]

By June 1954, Slikkers had started thinking more about his future and what he wanted to do next. The periodic work stoppages due to labor strikes, combined with the success with his after-hours boat building business, finally influenced his move away from Chris-Craft. When asked how much of an impact his years at Chris-Craft had on him, Slikkers thoughtfully remarked, "I often think of those nine years, almost ten years that I worked for them. No doubt it was a beginning of my boat building career. No question about it. If I had not done that, I don't think I would have ever [gone] into the boat business."[225]

By January 1955, the twenty-seven-year-old Slikkers had left the training ground of Chris-Craft and began making boats full time on his own. His duel-cockpit SlickCraft brand runabouts were made out of mahogany plywood decks and molded plywood hulls purchased from United States Molded Shapes Inc. "I paid my bills, and I had $5,000 left....And that was what I started the company with." Slikkers rented a small building with an upstairs apartment and a vacant space below for making boats at 791 South Washington Avenue in Holland.[226]

In February 1955, Slikkers settled his wife, Dolores, and two children, David and Robert, into an upstairs apartment of the building that made up the boat factory and began building his first official SlickCraft model year of molded plywood runabouts. There, Dolores served as the treasurer and secretary for the company, as well as mother to the growing family. During that same year, Slikkers made the critical decision to experiment with a new material that had been used to build boats since the 1940s: fiberglass.[227]

SlickCraft brand boats brochure, 1956. *S2 Yachts Inc. Collection.*

During the 1955 model year, Slikkers and his brother Paul, hired away from the local Chris-Craft plant, built thirty-five boats, an ambitious number for his small company.[228] As the company continued to make boats, Slikkers's friends, still employed at the Chris-Craft plant and Mac Bay Boat Company, frequently visited him and inquired about his progress as an entrepreneur. Over time, Slikkers hired many of these men and women because they showed a desire to work in a small, family-oriented plant—a place where craftsmen were valued and management endeavored to build and sell quality boats.

In December 1955, Slikkers contracted with local fiberglass boat builder Clyde Poll to build fifty hulls for his fledgling company. Slikkers received the hulls from Poll a few at a time and had his employees apply paint to them, as colored gel coat was not used by Poll yet. His crew then added mahogany wood decks, chrome deck hardware and seats that were produced by a local upholstering company like AutoTop.[229] The final result was either a fourteen-foot Caribbean or Cubana model, depending on the options the customer requested. The Keywester and Bermuda models were also fourteen-foot but built of molded plywood.

The 1957 models were built exclusively of molded plywood ranging in size from thirteen to fifteen feet.[230] Later that same year, Slikkers contracted with Zeeland-based fiberglass manufacturer Camfield Fiberglas Plastics Inc. to make between twenty-five and fifty fiberglass hulls and decks for the 1958 model year, even while he was experimenting and training his workers to perfect the skills needed to build their own fiberglass boats in the future. Those models included the integrated color in the gel coat for the first time. Later on, some deck molds were designed to simulate the striped deck look of the wood decked models. Although more color choices were available, like black, white, light green or salmon, the primary hull color was white. The company also continued to offer molded plywood models, ranging from fifteen to seventeen feet.[231] That same year, Slikkers also began experimenting with an alternative propulsion system for his boats by building a prototype inboard/outboard from one of his molded plywood hulls powered by a newly produced vertically mounted inboard engine, known as the Fageol V-I-P (vertical inboard power). Subsequent experiments with an inboard/outboard propulsion system in the early 1960s would change how Slick Craft built and sold boats.

Following the 1958 model year, Slikkers brought the fiberglass construction phase of the production line under his direct supervision and used his own designs and tested techniques for building a few of the 1959 models. Those models were constructed of a fiberglass hull at a plant located at 9 West Seventh Street, used at one time for the building of Mac Bay Boat Company boats, and then shipped to the Washington Avenue plant, where they were equipped with a mahogany wood deck, hardware, steering controls and seating. The company still made the molded plywood hulls in the sixteen- and seventeen-foot range, but as the year progressed, Slikkers came to understand that fiberglass boats in the same lengths were the future and that making the boats at his plant was the way to proceed.

The next decade for Slick Craft Boat Company would be one of continued growth in the building of fiberglass boats and the end of producing molded plywood boats. The company never looked back and headed into the future with every completed hull that left the factory.

Chapter 6

THE 1960s

Throughout the 1960s, the boat building industry underwent years of boom and bust in sales and production. Many smaller companies failed in the wake of low sales years, while others cut back on employees and increased their marketing to consumers or hired outside sales representatives. Some became targets for acquisition as larger companies sought to diversify their product offerings and increase profits.

CHRIS-CRAFT CORPORATION

On February 11, 1960, the Smith family, made up of fifty-four family shareholders, agreed to sell the Chris-Craft Corporation to NAFI Corporation for a reported sum of $40 million. The Chris-Craft sale was finalized on April 5, 1960.[232]

In the early 1960s, the Holland plant started making cruisers in the forty- to forty-two-foot range on a permanent basis and continued the manufacturing of the plywood Cavalier Division under plant manager Bill Jacobs, who had been appointed in 1960. That same year, Russ Fredericks was promoted to vice-president of Holland Divisions. While a new era for the corporation and dramatic changes in boat styling, there were only subtle changes in continuity and management.[233] The real change came from outside the company with the popularity of fiberglass as the material

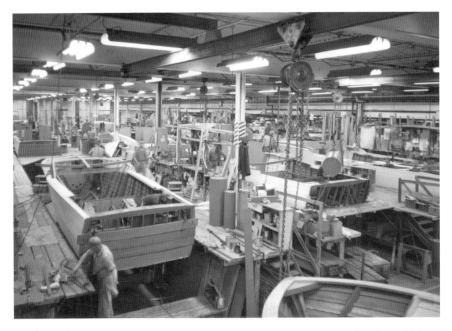

Chris-Craft Corporation Holland plant assembly line, 1958. *Roger MacLeod Collection, Holland Museum Archives and Research Library.*

of choice for consumers seeking larger boats that lasted longer with much less maintenance.

While the Chris-Craft Corporation had been creating small fiberglass parts for its boats since the mid-1950s, it found itself lagging behind competitors who were building complete boats in the early 1960s. The Holland plant and its employees were chosen to get the company back in the game. In 1963, the plugs, molds and ancillary tooling for the thirty-eight-foot Commander model was completed under the direction of Vice-President in charge of Manufacturing and Engineering A.W. McKerer and engineer Chris Smith. A new freestanding building was added to the north of the main building to construct the fiberglass hull, deck and parts, raising the plant complex footprint to 339,963 square feet. This new building separated not only the potential for fire from the volatile chemicals from the main building but also the smell, which many employees did not like. The few who did work with the fiberglass boat building process included many women, who according to Chris Smith did a better job of laying up the fiberglass and smoothing out the air bubbles and wrinkles once the liquid resin was applied.[234] Once the parts had been made, each was transferred to the nearby Roamer plant for assembly and completion so as not to disrupt the wood boat construction in the main wood boat plant building. This would be the last hull designed by McKerer, and it was an excellent one. The Commander 38 was introduced in the 1964 model year and went on to become a success, leading to tooling for six new designs with top side variations in only a four-year period at the Holland plant.[235] The construction of these new medium-sized cruiser fiberglass boats soon replaced the lagging wooden boats as demand by consumers moved away from wood and increased the profits of the company steadily through the middle part of the 1960s.[236]

In 1966, labor troubles returned to the Holland plant with a March 18 strike by hourly employees. The nearby Roamer Yachts plant went on strike in early May of that year.[237]

With the fast-moving conversion from wood to fiberglass boat construction, Chris-Craft became even more attractive to potential buyers. In late 1967, the company, known as Chris-Craft Industries Inc. since 1962, was taken over by a group of investors headed up by Herbert J. Siegal and merged with Baldwin-Montrose Inc. With it came enormous change that forever altered the course of the company and the job security of its employees. In 1968, the runabout plant at Cadillac closed due to slow sales in small wooden runabouts and the age of the building. The next year, Coll retired as president of the corporation after leading it and both of the Holland plants to years of success. Because of Coll and his successors, the dedicated and skilled workforce continued to be successful at the updated and efficient facility building modern, well-crafted fiberglass boats, while orders for wooden boats continued to diminish throughout the industry.[238]

ROAMER STEEL BOAT COMPANY DIVISION OF CHRIS-CRAFT CORPORATION

In 1960, the Roamer Steel Boat Company division introduced four sizes in various styles, ranging in size from thirty-one to fifty-five feet. Plant manager Michael Potter left Holland to become the assistant to the president of the corporation, Harry H. Coll, coordinating the executive functions at the new corporate headquarters in Pompano Beach. Potter was replaced at Roamer by William Sanford, a former engineer for the division.[239]

The next year, as the Aluminum Association celebrated the seventy-fifth anniversary of the metal's creation, Roamer was working to create its

Roamer Boat Division boat brochure, 1962. *Roamer Yachts Division of Chris-Craft Corporation Collection.*

first aluminum boat, an all new twenty-seven-foot express cruiser model. The hull sections were prefabricated, some stretch-formed on presses to achieve a flattering flare in the hull shape, and assembled on a jig where they were electrically welded into a single unit over longitudinal framing. The same year, the division was renamed the Roamer Yachts Division of the Chris-Craft Corporation and used the phrase "styled in steel and aluminum" in company advertising.[240] By 1965, the company was building three models in aluminum, ranging in size from thirty-seven to fifty-seven feet.[241]

By 1973, the Roamer Yachts Division of Chris-Craft Industries was building fiberglass boats only, starting at fifty-five feet and customized to customer specifications, according to plant manager Gite Van Kampen and engineer Chris Smith.[242] Production was transferred from the 186,829-square-foot Holland plant to Florida in 1975 and ended completely in 1979.[243]

SLICK CRAFT BOAT COMPANY

For the 1960 model year, the Slick Craft Boat Company moved the fiberglass production out of the small six-thousand-square-foot plant at 791 South Washington Avenue to one at 13 West Seventh Street. Boats were then transported back to the South Washington Avenue plant for final assembly and shipping. After the Seventh Street plant was deemed too small, a larger plant on Van Dyke Street, located on Holland's north side, was used.[244] That same year, the company eliminated all its molded plywood models and offered only fiberglass models.[245]

The 1961 model year brought with it the last of the historic wood-decked models. The sixteen-foot Premiere incorporated a brand-new V-hull design, which transitioned SlickCraft brand models to a more modern style. This new hull design was used again the next year as the company focused exclusively on fiberglass hulls and decks, to great financial reward.[246]

In 1962, the company moved production a few blocks farther south to a leased former skating rink, located at 1145 South Washington Avenue, while also retaining the original seventy- by one-hundred-foot building for offices.[247] There, Slikkers's growing staff, including his teenage son, David, enjoyed a much larger building, totaling twenty thousand square feet. This building would be expanded two more times, totaling forty-two thousand square feet by 1965.[248] In addition to physical expansion, the company hired two individuals who would be very important to expanding boat sales. Slikkers hired successful boat salesman Robert C. Egan, from outside the family, who promised to set up a network and drive up sales throughout the country. Egan had left the troubled Lancaster, Pennsylvania–based Skee-Craft Boat Company. Prior to Egan joining the company and representing the Eastern Division of the United States, Slick Craft had employed other independent representatives, like the Robert B. Hamilton Company based in Canandaigua, New York, which would visit dealers in particular parts of the United States and abroad and convince them to carry an inventory of SlickCraft brand boats. Prior to the hiring of independent representatives, Slikkers had served as sales manager for the company and dealt directly with customers.[249]

After a short time with the company, Egan initiated the Direct Dealer Agreement program for the company, cutting out the independent representatives and giving specific geographical sales territories to the dealers as long as they made an initial purchase of so many boats and carried a specific number of boats at all times.[250] This approach to sales

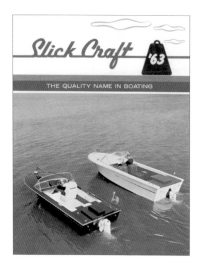

Slick Craft Boat Company's 1963 brochure. *S2 Yachts Inc. Collection.*

allowed the company to better plan for rates of production, purchase supplies in certain amounts per specific periods, print brochures, place advertising and have working capital to keep the whole process running smoothly. Slikkers also sought additional design assistance when he hired Ed Wennersten away from Chris-Craft with a substantial raise in pay and a promise to play a key role in the research and development area.[251] Slikkers further solidified family involvement, employing his three brothers—Gerald, Paul and Dennis—to oversee the design and production of the boats.[252]

From 1962 forward, the company used only fiberglass to build its boats, marking a huge change in the company's history. This change allowed Slikkers and his design team to create more colorful, safe, durable and less expensive outboard- and inboard/outboard-driven boats for consumers tired of maintaining wooden boats and hungry for new designs that molded fiberglass designs provided. Slikkers did not follow other boat manufacturers inspired by the automotive industry. His designs were clean, classic and useful to families. By October 1962, the eighteen-footers came with the relatively new technology of the inboard/outboard motor (I/O).[253]

In 1963, after the new propulsion system worked out its early design problems, Slikkers introduced the inboard/outboard motor as an option on three of his company's nine model line. With this new technology and the proven outboard line of boats, company production grew, and the business continued to expand to include its first cabin cruiser model.

With the larger facility in place and domestic sales booming, international sales soon followed in countries like Sweden, Switzerland and Spain. Slikkers was impressed with Egan's impact on both domestic and international boat sales and promoted him to vice-president of sales for the company.[254] To boost foreign sales to Canada, and possibly avoid import tax, a production facility agreement was arranged with Grew Boats Limited, located in Penetanguishene, Ontario, Canada, in 1964. The arrangement allowed Slick Craft to send a mold to Grew that was the same as the mold used in Holland, to make boats branded with the Grew name.[255] In 1969, a similar arrangement was made with Vator Oy in Helsinki, Finland. These two companies produced a limited line of boats from molds designed by the Slick Craft Boat Company. Vator Oy branded its boats only with the SlickCraft name.[256] To better transport boats to domestic dealers, Slikkers tasked his brother Dennis with designing and building the semi-trailers that would transport SlickCraft brand boats far and wide. Later, he would become a salesman and retired as the vice-president of sales for S2 Yachts Inc. in 1995.[257]

In 1964, Egan helped introduce a sales change to the way the boat models were named and hulls numbered, to better track each hull for ordering, production, delivery and any warranty claims. This change eventually evolved into the changing of the formal names of each model in 1965 model year; for example, the fourteen-foot Sun Sport became the SS-140.[258]

In July 1965, the company announced the purchase of an eighteen-acre site in Holland's new South Side Industrial Park at 500 East Thirty-Second Street for the construction of a new 65,000-square-foot manufacturing plant. The new plant included administrative offices and a warehouse for ninety completed boats larger than 23 feet, like the larger cabin cruiser models. The plant, designed by industrial firm Richardson/Smith, was completed in November, giving the company a total of 100,000 square feet of space.[259] The plant at 1145 South Washington Avenue was used to manufacture boats from 15 to 23 feet in length and house the administrative offices and engineering department.[260] Slikkers predicted that the new plant would allow him to build more boats, ranging in price from $1,095 to $7,000, with more workers, quoted then as nine hundred boats per year built by fifty employees through one hundred dealers.[261]

SlickCraft brand boats were so well respected that in late 1967, Bill Wittig, then head of sales for the Century Boat Company, located in Manistee, Michigan, contracted with Slikkers to build a boat that was the fiberglass version of both the fifteen- and sixteen-foot Century Resorter models, which became the sixteen-foot fiberglass Cheetah model. Slick Craft workers used a modified wooden Resorter hull as a plug to make a mold for the project. Then they made about thirty of the avocado green hulls at the 1145 South Washington Avenue plant and shipped them to Manistee along with the mold. In early 1968, Slikkers traveled to Manistee and trained the Century employees to work with the tools, fiberglass and resin to build the Cheetah model and order supplies for future fiberglass boat production.[262] A major change to the 1967 SlickCraft line included the introduction of the cathedral/tri-hull design, which was supposed to offer a more stable ride but also caused the boats to ride over the waves, adding to the rough ride on water with any wave heights.

In April 1968, the company announced that an additional eighty thousand square feet would be added to the East Thirty-Second Street plant, more than doubling the existing plant footprint for his 102 employees, including those who worked at the older 1145 South Washington Avenue plant. The expansion, completed in December by Jack Lamar's company using many other local subcontractors, was caused by not only a need for more production space of the larger and taller models, like the new *SC-285* twenty-eight-foot cabin cruiser, but also more space for office staff in a newly designed mezzanine floor.[263] By September, the company had purchased another seven acres to add even more production and warehouse space, bringing the East Thirty-Second Street property total to twenty-five acres.[264] To oversee its ever-growing labor force, the company hired longtime boat company human resources professional Gerry VandeVusse in November. VandeVusse was eminently qualified for the job after serving with the Chris-Craft Corporation from 1942 to 1968.[265]

In May 1969, the company announced a formal open house to the people of Holland to visit the newly completed addition and improvements to the 150,000-square-foot East Thirty-Second Street plant with a full-page advertisement in the *Holland Sentinel*.[266] Times were indeed good for the company in 1969 after a decade of change in construction materials, new designs and power options and explosive growth in sales and production facilities.

Throughout the late 1960s, the SlickCraft brand name, which was officially registered as a trademark in April 1969, became synonymous with quality and affordability; it also attracted the attention of conglomerates interested in acquiring boat building companies in attempts to diversify their holdings into the recreation market and attract potential stockholders.[267] So it was not a surprise when New York State–based American Machine and Foundry Corporation (AMF) approached Leon Slikkers about selling his company for a large sum of money. In September 1969, after much thought and prayer, the Slikkers family decided to sell the company to AMF.[268] As part of the sale agreement, Slikkers would stay on as president of the Slickcraft Division of AMF.

MICHIGAN FIBERGLASS COMPANY

Michigan Fiberglass Company was started by Lawrence Valentine Meyering in 1960.[269] Meyering was born in Chicago in 1907 and graduated from the University of Wisconsin in 1928, earning a Juris Doctor degree from Northwestern University in 1931.[270] In 1942, Meyering left his position as a law associate with Frank C. Rathje and moved with his wife, Gervaise, from Highland Park, Illinois, to work for the Grand Haven, Michigan–based Camfield Fiberglass Plastics Inc., manufactures and marketers of electrical appliances, as well as molded plywood and plastic (fiberglass) products. There he rose to the position of president and treasurer in 1947. Meyering lead the company's entry into reinforced plastics along with Carl E. Holmes.[271] The company moved to nearby Zeeland, Michigan, in 1955.

After encountering some internal strife with management in 1959, Meyering left the company. Not long after leaving Camfield, Meyering contacted former Camfield coworker Henry Kort about his desire to start up a boat company and to inquire whether Kort would be interested in

Michigan Fiberglass Company employees applying fiberglass and resin to a boat mold, circa 1960. *Lawrence V. Meyering Collection.*

Michigan Fiberglass Company boat plant assembly line, circa 1960. *Lawrence V. Meyering Collection.*

becoming his facility manager. After Kort accepted the job, Meyering instructed him to prepare a rented warehouse located at 471 Howard Avenue near Aniline Drive. That building once served as Plant no. 5 for the Holland Furnace Company and was owned by Chemitron when Meyering saw to the transfer of fiberglass molds and equipment from Parsons Corporation of Traverse City, for Michigan Fiberglass to use as a subcontractor to build the Lake 'n Sea Boats line of boats.[272] Parsons made the move to subcontract the construction part of the boats to reduce costs. After the molds arrived, Meyering and Kort, also in charge of manufacturing, began the process of building the Lake 'n Sea line speedboats with a crew of thirty-five to fifty people. A representative for Chemitron, John Schutten, remembered the Michigan Fiberglass Company employees not being able to provide the same quality of boat making as the Parsons staff when it came to proper fiberglass boat construction. Many of the boat hulls were ruined when separated from the mold due to bad releasing agents and stacked up outside the building awaiting disposal.[273]

In December 1960, the Parsons Corporation announced that it was suspending the manufacture of the boat line for the 1961 model year to allow its engineers and designers time to create new designs and manufacturing techniques for the 1962 model year.[274] In 1961, the company sold the unsold boats, molds, equipment and brand to Michigan Fiberglass Company.[275] With badly made boat hulls and bills piling up, Meyering vacated the factory building, ended manufacturing of the Lake 'n Sea speedboat line and moved his operation to two rented buildings in nearby Borculo, Michigan, located at the southeast corner of Port Sheldon Road and Ninety-Sixth Avenue. At the Borculo location, the company, now employing about ten employees, made green fiberglass canoes for the Boy Scouts of America organization, including a small twelve-foot, four-inch sailboat model filled with polystyrene called the Porpoise and an eleven-foot polystyrene foam boat covered in protective paint called the Beachcomber.[276] The Beachcomber model was also marketed by Meyering under the business name L.V.M. Associates Inc. of Coopersville, Michigan, but little is known about this business venture.[277] The company remained there until 1963 building boats, many of which were sold through dealers like Grand Rapids businessman Richard Levy. Meyering, while working for Camfield, had met and sold fiberglass saucer-shaped snow sleds to Levy for his mail order catalogue. Even though the company made lots of boats, estimated at five to six hundred, many of the Beachcomber boats were recalled for manufacturing and design flaws, and financial losses mounted for Meyering.[278]

In 1963, Kort purchased the rights and equipment to make the canoe, selling about 120 before liquidating. Levy and Morrie Kleiman purchased the inventory and equipment associated with the Porpoise model and built them under the Molded Products Company name at 3125 Madison Avenue Southeast, Grand Rapids, Michigan.[279] Meyering retired in 1972 and passed away on October 9, 1993, in Comstock Park, Michigan.[280]

Chapter 7

THE 1970s

The 1970s brought additional changes to the boat building landscape in Holland as one conglomerate continued onward, building larger and larger boats out of fiberglass, while another sought to build more boats with less money, forcing a pioneer in the industry to create a new company and leave one behind. The decade also saw a husband-and-wife team pursue a dream of building small boats, only to watch it fail and destroy family relationships forever.

CHRIS-CRAFT INDUSTRIES

By model year 1971, just a few wood boats were being built by Chris-Craft Industries. Ironically, the president of the corporation asked Holland plant manager Bill Jacobs to build one of those remaining models, the fifty-seven-foot Constellation. To build that model, production lines eight and nine had to be joined to accommodate it, the largest model ever built, at that time, in the Holland plant. It is believed that only four boats of this model were ever built at the plant before the last one. The last wooden boat ever built by the company shipped from the Holland plant in 1972.[281]

The Holland plant continued to build fiberglass boats for another sixteen years as the corporation saw presidents come and go, along with their ideas for making the company great again. In 1978, Russ Fredericks, hired in 1939 as the plant's employment manager, retired as vice-president of the Holland and Roamer operations after forty years of service. He passed away in January 1979.[282] Bill Jacobs, originally hired in 1939 as a rough carpenter to help build the plant, then promoted to hull department foreman and, finally, plant manager, also retired in 1978. Chris Smith, namesake and grandson of the company founder, came to the Holland plant in 1946 and retired from the company in 1986.[283]

In 1981, G. Dale Murray, a coal industry magnate, purchased the Chris-Craft boating operations and renamed the company Murray Chris-Craft.[284] In many people's minds, Murray saved the company from disappearing completely from the industry. During his time as chairman of the company, working with board members like Dick Genth, Ed McMahon, General Alexander Haig, F. Lee Bailey and Leon Finley, Murray steered company sales from $25 million to nearly $200 million in 1988.[285] Later that same year, on December 9, Murray Industries filed for Chapter 11 bankruptcy protection. Even though the Chris-Craft name was purchased and boats continued to be made in other locations with modern manufacturing facilities, the aging Holland plant was not included, most likely due to the cost of bringing it up to modern production capability. Others have speculated that the presence of an active labor union, like the Chris-Craft plant in Bellingham, Washington, might have left the plant out of the purchase. The last boat produced at the Holland plant, an Amerosport cruiser, left on Friday, January 27, 1989, with seventy-five remaining employees looking on. The company was purchased by Outboard Marine Corporation (OMC) later that year.[286] The plant, renamed 100 Aniline Building, remained under the ownership of Murray Industries Inc. and was rebranded as a mini-industrial park for small, growing businesses that leased space from Commercial Industrial Real Estate Office (CIRO). Murray Industries also operated a small boat building and repair business in a fifty-thousand-square-foot building on the site. Once the bankruptcy proceedings were completed in 1992, the property was turned over to Interredec, which was Murray Industries' largest creditor. The property was sold to CIRO representative Roger MacLeod and business partner Phillip Dressel in July 1999 and continued as before.[287]

The Holland plant had made more than ten thousand wooden boats alone during its long history in a facility that in 1988 covered 400,000 square feet of floor space. That successful run was attributed to three objectives: quality, on-schedule production and low cost. For the company, the Holland plant was a financial and operating success, crucial in setting the pattern for its tremendous growth from the 1940s through the 1960s. The Holland community benefited from the progressive, stable and clean industry the plant offered. The employees benefited from job security and an atmosphere to exhibit their talents and dedication to hard work. For many, it was a lifelong career with promotions.[288]

SLICKCRAFT DIVISION OF AMF CORPORATION

In the fall of 1969, under the leadership of Chairman of the Board Rodney C. Gott, American Machine and Foundry Corporation (AMF) purchased the Slick Craft Boat Company.[289] Leon Slikkers stayed on as president of the Slickcraft Division of AMF Corporation in an effort to keep the same quality of workmanship that had built and improved the company since 1954. In 1971, AMF expanded its recreational boat lines when it acquired Robalo fishing boats, which were made at a Sanford, Florida plant. The console boat design was perfected by a number of designers in the mid-1960s, like C. Raymond Hunt of Boston Whaler fame.

In November 1972, the company expanded across the street with a new, separate building measuring 150 by 500 feet to provide space for the manufacturing of larger boats and to house the research and development group. At the time, Leon Slikkers's title had been expanded to include AMF division vice-president and Slickcraft unit executive, while his brother Paul was listed as vice-president of production. Both men were under pressure to cut costs at the plant, which meant cost over quality, and that was too much for both men.[290]

SlickCraft division of AMF Corporation administrative staff, April 1973. *SlickCraft Division of AMF Collection.*

In late November 1973, the *Holland City News* reported the resignation of Leon Slikkers from the boat company division and his replacement by Richard J. Camarota as vice-president and general manager.[291]

In 1981, AMF Inc., which had grown to be known as a leisure equipment maker, was purchased by Irwin L. Jacobs, a Minneapolis investor and controller of Minstar Inc., for $300 million. After the purchase, the Holland division, licensed as AMF Powerboat of AMF Inc. since 1972, stopped making boats.[292]

S2 YACHTS INC.

After Leon Slikkers left AMF, he immediately began experimenting with a fiberglass sailboat design that would allow him to build boats but not violate his non-compete clause with AMF to build powerboats, which was due to expire in 1976.[293] On February 18, 1974, S2 Yachts, which stands for "Slikkers Second Time Around," was founded.[294] "I have an interest in sailboats. I just felt there was an opportunity to apply some of the processes that I had found in production, to apply them to sailboat industry would be advantageous," Slikkers remembered in a 2002 interview.[295] The new company contracted with naval architect Arthur Edmonds on three models: two twenty-six-foot models and one twenty-three-foot model. While Slikkers and his fifteen-member team, including sons David and Robert, worked out of the same small plant at 13 West Seventh Street, used years before to make SlickCraft brand boats, he was also building a seventy-two-thousand-square-foot plant at 725 East Fortieth Street. The new plant initially employed fifty-three employees when completed and made ready for production of sailboats.[296]

Robert Egan, who left AMF in 1974, brought in Richard Thede, from the Chicago-area Thede Marine, to help sell the new sailboat line. Thede started selling Slick Craft–built boats back in 1963, and Slikkers consulted with Thede early on when he decided to build and sell sailboats for the first time. Thede was dealer no. 001 for the S2 Yachts sailboat line for many years before Slikkers hired him as sales manager and later as a part-time sales representative.[297] After a few years, it became apparent that the shoal draft keel sailboat needed to be improved to become a better-performing sailboat. In response, S2 Yachts worked with Chicago design firm Graham & Schalageter to build a new twenty-six-foot model with

S2 Yachts Inc. sailboat brochure, 1974.
S2 Yachts Inc. Collection.

a vertical retracting keel, transported via a trailer—a good performer and consumers liked it. The company produced this design, in different lengths, until 1987.[298]

Two years after introducing the sailboat line, the company decided that the sail segment of the industry wasn't as big as it had thought, so it entered the powerboat industry and added the luxury Tiara Yachts powerboat line. In 1977, the company introduced the Pursuit series of fishing boats.[299] In 1979, the company doubled the capacity of the plant and expanded all product lines, including the S2 sailboats and Tiara powerboats, adding the Grand Slam performance sailboat series.[300] The relatively "new" company ended the 1970s on a high note and prepared for a new decade and new growth.

LOVECRAFT BOAT COMPANY

The Lovecraft Boat Company was a small boat manufacturer founded by Dale Love in January 1970 with a capital of $50,000 in Dale and his wife Yvonne's three-car garage at 1258 Graafschap Road, in Holland.[301] The company made two models of a small ten- by five-foot fiberglass catamaran paddle boat, called Puppy Love. One model was engine powered and one foot pedal powered. The engine-powered model, priced at $1,395, was driven by a four-cycle three-and-a-half-horsepower Briggs & Stratton engine that pushed it to a top speed of eight knots for a maximum two and a half hours with one quart of fuel. A convertible canvas top and trailer were optional. The company also made a third model called Puppy Love Pontoon, powered by an outboard motor up to seven and a half horsepower maximum that measured fourteen by five feet.[302]

The couple started out small in building up the company. Dale quit his job as a designer for houseboat builder Rollie Peterson in nearby Douglas, Michigan, to try building his own boats.[303] At the time, Yvonne was working for SlickCraft building boats out of fiberglass using large molds. With the help of coworker Russ Van Order, Yvonne laid up the first crude mold for the much smaller boat from the plywood prototype created by Dale in their garage. A final fiberglass mold was then made for a fiberglass prototype.[304]

With a fiberglass prototype made and tested, Dale rented out the basement of a nearby cement building at 642 West Forty-Eighth Street owned by Herk Knoll and moved the operation out of their garage. At the new site, Yvonne, Van Order and Dale started making the small fiberglass pontoon boats.

Soon, his retired parents, Vern and Eunice Love, became investors in the company and moved into an apartment near Dale and Yvonne in Graafschap. Dale was excited to work with his father in the business.[305] With the company up and running, Yvonne continued working for SlickCraft during the day and spraying gel coat and laying up fiberglass and resin at night with Van Order. Dale removed the cured hulls during the day and completed the boat for sale. Many sales were completed by Dale's father, a retired meat packinghouse owner and salesman. As more orders came in for the boats, Dale hired John Peterson to help sell and deliver boats to even more customers.

By 1971, the Lovecraft Boat Company was doing very well, as competition in the small paddleboat market seemed to be nonexistent, according to Yvonne. Even with national competition, the company was doing so well that the newly built Disney World in Orlando, Florida, wanted the engine-powered version of the Lovecraft paddleboats in its park on opening day in October. After phone conversations went well, Dale and Yvonne made a few trips to Orlando, with a few demonstration models of their boat.[306]

The boats were built in the little factory and outfitted with four-cycle three-and-a-half-horsepower Briggs & Stratton engines purchased from Ed Voss's Reliable Sports in Holland.[307] To deliver the boats to Orlando, Dale built a special trailer that would hold up to six boats at a time, and either Dale and Yvonne or Peterson made the deliveries. Yvonne and Dale were there on opening day when Disney World debuted with thirty Lovecraft-built boats.[308]

With the Disney contract to be filled and other customers, Dale and Yvonne needed more room to expand the company. Dale contacted Herk Knoll and rented a long, old chicken coop across the street from the existing factory, creating an assembly line and an office. Soon, the couple decided to have Yvonne quit Slickcraft and work for Lovecraft when needed. In the meantime, Dale's dad was also selling.[309]

With more boats selling, more help was needed. The company hired Yvonne's brother-in-law, Sam Phillips, away from the local Thermotron factory. Dale hired former coworker Phil Clark away from the River Queen boat company in Douglas. Soon, all the employees and their spouses lived and worked in the small village of Graafschap near the factory. Even with brisk sales and production, the company was in trouble, as Dale and Yvonne's business partnership began to erode over some employee practices and overall control of the company. Peterson left the company over dwindling sales. As sales lagged, Dale's parents continued to pour money into the company to keep it afloat, believing it was a good product and that if it could just get going, they all would make some money off of it.[310] Feeling the pressure building, Dale sought the advice of a local banker, who suggested he take on a business partner or go out of business. Reluctantly, Dale entered into partnership with Bill Mouw, owner of Glamour Pools of the Midwest in Holland. Mouw immediately sold off all the company assets, as the partners planned a conversion to a vacuum-forming boat building process versus hand layup, as had been done previously.[311]

With the new boat construction plan failing, creditors seeking payment and his parents with no more money to invest, Dale was faced with bankruptcy. Representatives from the bank came to foreclose on everything associated with the company, including tools and his favorite GMC truck that he had painted coral and white, just like his boats, in 1972.[312]

Forest and Russell Homkes purchased the assets of the company from the bank and produced the paddle boats under the Ruskraft Company at 935 South Washington Avenue in Holland for a short time, in a building that had originally housed the Roamer brand boat operation.[313] There, about twenty boats were made and sent to Hawaii. The new company lasted about eighteen months, making both the motorized and pedal-powered models with the coral-and-white color scheme. "Since we could not create a viable dealer network and because other brands were charging less and cutting into our business we got out of it and dissolved the company," recalled Russell Homkes in 2002.[314] Eventually, Gary Holt acquired the molds for the boats and then sold them to Zeeland-based Moes Enterprise, makers of fiberglass canoes, in the 1980s. The Moes brothers, Dale and Jim, gave the molds back to Yvonne and Dale Love's son, Randy, in 2010.

Eventually, Dale sold the Lovecraft trademark, which he had retained when the company was legally dissolved, to Rockford businessman Henry Timmer, but it does not appear that any more boats were ever made under the Lovecraft brand.[315]

Chapter 8

THE 1980s AND BEYOND

The ever-changing trends in the economy and conglomerates in the pleasure boating industry during the last fifty years have worked against the development of new boat building companies in Holland. Only those with creative design, a skilled workforce building quality boats, sensitivity to consumer demand, loyalty and financial capital have survived.

S2 YACHTS INC.

In 1983, S2 Yachts Inc. purchased the Slickcraft brand name from AMF, which had stopped producing that line of boats in 1980 when it closed the Holland plant. A few years later, the Slickcraft line was separated from the Tiara line to create a smaller sport boat line and create two distinct lines for two distinct types of consumers. The company was unable to make the Slickcraft line as attractive to consumers as it had been in the 1960s, so it was replaced with a newly created Tiara Sportboats line in 1989. The new line was dropped in 1991 due to federal luxury tax and trouble distributing the line to dealers fast enough to make it profitable for either party.[316]

In 1983, the company decided to create a fishing boat model suited for the growing Great Lakes salmon fishery. The Pursuit series was created from a stripped-down version of the smaller Tiara line, more "fishy" and less "dressy." In July of that year, the company built a new seventy-five-thousand-square-foot boat plant in Fort Pierce, Florida, to build the smaller Tiara series boats, ranging in size from twenty to twenty-five feet. In the beginning, a few key employees—like Leon Slikkers, building project manager Paul Slikkers and personnel manager Gerry VandeVusse—traveled to and from the Florida plant to hire workers and get it up and running. Three longtime employees—Carlos Miranda, Sergio Orozco and Michael Sinden—relocated permanently to the area to work at the plant. The rest of the initial forty workers were hired locally.[317] Eventually, the Tiara/Slickcraft Sportboats line and the Pursuit line of fishing boats would also be built there and become a more familiar brand name with the saltwater fishermen. This move proved critical, as the brand would eventually sell approximately 85 percent of its boats to saltwater sailors.[318]

In 1984, Leon Slikkers became the chief executive officer of S2 Yachts Inc., and oldest son David Slikkers was named president of S2 Yachts Inc. That same year, construction was completed on a new 200,000-square-foot two-level addition, which brought the plant footprint to nearly 500,000 square feet.[319] The company also introduced the Tiara Yachts 3600 series of boats, historically one of its best-selling series.[320]

In 1986, the company reorganized its brand names to include separate dealer franchises for each product line, which now included Tiara Yachts, Pursuit Fishing Boats, Slickcraft Sportboats and S2 Sailboats.[321] A key management team was assembled for a second generation of growth that now included second-oldest son, Robert Slikkers, and third-oldest son, Thomas Slikkers, as product manager of the new Slickcraft Sportboats division. Together, the four divisions employed more than six hundred employees.[322]

In 1987, the Slickcraft product line expanded to include five new models, while the S2 Sailboat line ended with more than five thousand boats built, becoming one of the top five sailboat builders in the United States.[323] That same year, the 600th Tiara 3100 model rolled off the line in May, new sales records were established for the remaining three brand names and the team stood at more than five hundred employees.[324]

The following year, the company expanded its corporate facilities by doubling its engineering area, adding a corporate sportswear store and expanding the corporate entrance and lobby area. Again, new sales records were established for all three brand names, and the staff numbered 650 employees.[325]

In 1989, the company reintroduced the S2 twenty-six-foot sailboat on a limited-edition basis and made it available to consumers in 1990. That year also saw another record set for sales in all three brand names and staff rise to 780 employees.[326]

In the 1990s, the Slickcraft Sportboat was redesigned into the Tiara Sportboats line.[327] In the spring of 1992, the Tiara 3100 Open Classic hull no. 1,000 was completed, making it one of the best sellers for the company. That same year, the company redesigned and built new molds, at a cost of $750,000, and introduced a new version of the Tiara 3100 Open at the Fort Lauderdale Boat Show, at a base price of $126,180.[328] The company also introduced to consumers the Pursuit center console models. The slightly larger 2655 Pursuit center console went on to be named *Boating* magazine's 1992 Boat of the Year.[329]

In the spring of 1993, the company was one of approximately 350 major boat makers in the United States, making 457,000 boats. The new Tiara 2900 Open was introduced at the Fort Lauderdale Boat Show, and the 4300 Express was introduced to dealers in the fall. Each boat took almost twelve weeks to build, from fifty-three separate molds. With the repeal of the tax on luxury items costing more than $100,000 in August of that year, the Tiara division started selling more boats and looked forward to adding more employees to its 340-person workforce.[330] That same year, the Tiara Sportboats brand ended as S2 focused on the Tiara Yachts and Pursuit Fishing Boats product lines, ranging in size from nineteen and a half to thirty-one feet. The Pursuit brand also began its Total Quality Management Program and Total Company Education Program, based on the company's vision statement.[331]

In 1994, S2 Yachts Inc. celebrated its twentieth anniversary with an open house for all employees and their families. That same year, the company was selected as the winner in the manufacturing division of the MCI/ *Inc.* magazine's National Award for Positive Customer Service. Consumer demand for the S2 twenty-six-foot sailboat caused the company to produce the boats on a limited basis. As a new sales record was established for the Pursuit division, the company held its first Pursuit Offshore University for dealers and appointed Thomas Slikkers president of the division. Thomas had started assisting his father in the running of the plant in 2001. He was the third son, born in the apartment above the original South Washington Avenue plant. Thomas had begun his career at the company in 1976 as a janitor, just like his two older brothers, but in the new S2 Yachts plant. He worked his way through many jobs at the plant during his middle and high school years. Thomas started working in the accounting department in 1991[332] and left there in 1993 to work in the sales department—where

Tiara Yachts workers applying fiberglass and resin to a boat mold, circa 2000. *S2 Yachts Inc. Collection.*

he learned about the customer, dealers and the relationship between the two—before taking over for his father as the head of the Pursuit Fishing Boats line.[333]

In February 1995, the company established the company training program Tiara University, and its masters graduates went on to set new individual sales achievement records, along with the Pursuit division dealers.

In 1996, just over fifty years since founding the Slick Craft Boat Company, Leon Slikkers was named Entrepreneur of the Year in the manufacturing category for the State of Michigan. That same year, the company began construction on its ten-acre recreational park, and the Pursuit division set another new sales record. The Pursuit division also began a major 50,000-square-foot plant and 7,500-square-foot office space expansion at its Fort Pierce plant, which was completed the next year.[334]

In 1997, Leon Slikkers was inducted into the Michigan Boating Hall of Fame. The Tiara division debuted plans to introduce a division-wide cutting-edge wellness plan called SHIPSHAPE and construct a third production facility on the Atlantic coast within the next year. The company also began plans to build its first fifty-foot boat, the 5000 Express, in 1998. The Pursuit division set new sales records along with the Tiara division.[335]

In February 1998, the Pursuit division was also awarded its second Yamaha Motor Company's Sales and Marketing Achievement Award in as many years. The Tiara division's new Atlantic coast plant in Swansboro, North Carolina, opened in April, and the new 5000 Express was introduced to dealers, making it the largest boat offered to date. Both divisions set new sales records.[336]

The 1990s closed with Leon Slikkers being inducted into the National Marine Industry Hall of Fame in September 1999, joining Chris-Craft founder Christopher Columbus Smith.[337] That same year, the 500th Tiara division–built 3100 Open series hull was produced and delivered, and the first 5000 Express was completed at the new Swansboro manufacturing facility. Tiara Yachts was awarded the Best Boat Show Display at the Miami International Boat Show. In May, Pursuit received its third Yamaha Motor Company's Sales and Marketing Achievement Award and introduced the Continuous Improvement Plan at its plant. The decade closed with the S2 Yachts Inc. celebrating its twenty-fifth anniversary with a reception for all its 900 employees, 530 of whom worked at the Holland plant.[338]

The twenty-first century at S2 Yachts started with leadership changes. In August 2001, Leon Slikkers passed on the title of chief executive officer to his son David, who had been president since 1984. Son Robert, formerly senior vice-president of operations, was promoted to president of the Tiara Yachts division. Son Tom was promoted from vice-president of operations of the Pursuit Boats division to president of the division. Leon retained the title of chairman of the board. Employees of the company numbered about 1,000, with about 650 working at the Holland plant.[339] Once in place, David focused on three key areas to grow business for all divisions within the company: developing programs for dealers to sell boats, new product development and improving corporate performance within the industry by improving plant environment.[340]

The year 2004 marked the thirtieth anniversary of the founding of S2 Yachts Inc. In a newspaper interview, Leon fondly remembered starting the company at 13 West Seventh Street, where two sawhorses and a birch door served as his desk, with the excitement of starting a new boat building company based on Christian principles, commitment to excellence and stewardship to his employees and company. In 2004, the company's divisions were building about one thousand Pursuit brand boats, ranging in size from twenty-two to thirty-four feet and in price from $50,000 to $200,000, and five hundred Tiara brand yachts, some as big as fifty-two feet and prices starting at $1.1 million.[341]

The next year, the company announced the expansion of its Holland plant for the first time in twenty years, with a planned 283,000-square-foot $14 million building project that would boost its boat building capacity up to 56 feet by late 2006. Because the company had purchased additional acreage nearby, giving the company a total of eighty acres, the addition to two existing buildings was easily accomplished. They were also given a 50 percent, twenty-three-year tax abatement on the $12 million building construction and a 100 percent tax break on new equipment for the plant.[342] This expansion was in preparation for the closing of its Tiara division plant in Swansboro, due to a downturn in sales to its East Coast customers. That closing also allowed the Holland plant to expand its footprint and bring all Tiara line boat building under one roof again.

In 2008, the United States economy started its descent into what became known as the Great Recession, and S2 Yachts Inc. felt its effects. In response to the drop in sales of its Tiara Yachts and Pursuit Boats lines, David Slikkers founded a new company within the Holland plant to manufacture utility-scale wind turbine blades and other components out of fiberglass, thus entering the wind energy industry using fifty years of fiberglass boat construction experience. The new subsidiary of S2 Yachts Inc., Energetx Composites, received a $27.3 million tax break in June 2009 to energize the growth of the new company.[343] The new company continued receiving tax credits, job creation and stimulus funds, totaling $8.5 million, throughout 2009 and 2010 as leadership worked to keep the company profitable.[344] In April 2011, the company contracted to build the forty-four-foot Zeelander Z44 boats for Netherlands-based Zeelander Yachts as a subcontractor to offset the downturn in sales of its own Tiara Yachts line, while Energetx moved closer to producing components for clients.[345] It also built VanDutch brand boats as a subcontractor for the Netherlands-based Vanguard Dutch Marine Limited, from 2009 to 2013.[346]

Following the worst years of the recession, many boat building companies were out of business, but S2 Yachts was looking to redesign the boats that the next generation of customers wanted. Leading that move was Thomas Slikkers, appointed CEO and president of S2 Yachts Inc. in June 2012.[347]

S2 Yachts Inc. and its Tiara Yachts and Pursuit Boats lines continue to make history as a family-owned business in an industry dominated by conglomerates.

GRAND CRAFT BOATS, LLC

During the 1960s, classic wooden boats were nearing the end of their production as Fiberglass Reinforced Plastic (FRP) became the new standard for boat construction. In the 1970s, small boatyards started restoring older wooden boats and building replicas for customers unhappy with the look, ride and appeal of fiberglass boats. Customers wanted a boat with traditional styling, durable construction and modern performance technologies that were comfortable and easy to maintain. Macatawa Bay Boat Works of Holland, Michigan, was one of these pioneers.[348]

In 1979, Steven Northuis, his father and his grandfather founded the company known as Macatawa Bay Boat Works, located at 448 West Twenty-First Street, Holland, Michigan. The company built replica 1930 Chris-Craft twenty-four-foot triple-cockpit boats and restored all makes of wooden boats. His crew was made up of experienced craftsmen, many former employees of the local Chris-Craft boat factory, including brothers Chris and George Smith, grandsons of Christopher Columbus Smith, the founder of Chris-Craft. Chris Smith used an original 1930 model to loft the plans used for the Grand-Craft brand replica Chris-Craft brand twenty-four-foot boats, which were first produced in 1982 and priced at $29,000.[349] The next year, the company offered the Grand-Craft Custom 27, a ten-passenger classic based on the 1933 Chris-Craft design, as well as the twenty-four-foot model. Its brochure also mentioned that Chris-Craft retirees and young apprentices were now working at the factory, undoubtedly to meet the increased demand for replica wooden classics.

In 1983, Northuis introduced the twenty-three-foot Luxury Open-Cockpit model that was an original design for the company and one that caught the eye of actor Robert Redford. Redford eventually ordered the Grand-Craft twenty-three-foot Luxury Sport Custom with hardtop model from Northuis. During the building process, Redford visited the Holland boat shop to check on the upholstery color, seating arrangement and other specifications. Redford's visits were not unlike other Grand-Craft boat owners', who appeared periodically to check on the progress of their new boat, take in the aroma of the freshly worked mahogany wood, photograph the progress and discuss changes. When Northuis sold the company, Redford's boat was still under construction, as were many other orders from his three-model brochure of boats.

The Grand-Craft division of Macatawa Bay Boat Works was purchased from the Northuis family in 1984 by husband and wife Richard "Dick" and

Early Grand-Craft Corporation brochure. *Grand Craft Boats, LLC, Collection.*

Marti Sligh of Holland and incorporated as Grand-Craft Corporation.[350] Dick grew up around the water in Holland and enjoyed putting on waterskiing shows on Lake Macatawa with his brothers, sister and friends. Dick was also a wood boat enthusiast of long standing, having worked on wood boats since his childhood days and owned a marina (Sligh Marine) on Lake Charlevoix in East Jordan, Michigan, that specialized in the care of wood boats.[351]

While Marti came into the wood boat building business from an academic background, she quickly took to partnering with Dick in making the company a success. Together, they put in many long hours, weeks and months developing a marketing plan, taking in restoration work and eventually modifying some features in the classic runabouts, as well as developing a new twenty-foot model that had an all-new look. This model was called the twenty-foot Sport Runabout and was designed by Dick. The structure of their boats was much like those of decades past, using seven-eighths- by three-inch mahogany for hull frames, with the hull being laid up with two layers of quarter-inch mahogany. The first layer was put on diagonally to the chine (the corner location where the side of the boat meets the bottom) and then epoxied to a second layer of horizontal planking. Then the inside of the boat was saturated in epoxy resin, while the exterior side received stain and between twelve and eighteen coats of varnish. This is referred to as the cold-molded mahogany approach, using the wet epoxy saturation technique (WEST), and is still in use today.[352]

Other modern improvements included using stainless steel fasteners in some areas, while using time-tested silicon bronze fasteners in others. For their larger boats, four layers of mahogany were used on the bottom and three on the sides to further strengthen their construction. This type of construction allowed the Slighs to offer a lifetime guarantee of workmanship and materials for their boats and prove that wooden boats built with contemporary construction materials were a viable alternative to the proliferation of fiberglass boats.[353] Soon it became the company's most popular model due to its solid mahogany construction, excellent performance on the water and contemporary good looks. It was so well designed that Robert Redford traded in his original twenty-three-foot Grand-Craft boat for this newer design. At the time, it was the only twenty-foot Sport with a fiberglass hardtop. Redford's first boat was returned to Grand-Craft, restored and sold to a new owner.[354] The company added a double-cockpit version of this model to further satisfy customer demand. In addition to offering classic and contemporary designs in a fine-looking mahogany boat, the Slighs and their craftsmen worked with customers to customize features and upholstery color combinations.[355]

In 1987, the Slighs introduced their twenty-foot Custom Classic model at a special preview event in Holland's Kollen Park. The double-cockpit, triple-tone interior and blond decking model was designed by Dick for the 1988 model year.[356] They also introduced a company newsletter to keep their customers connected with the company and abreast of new services and boat models and to introduce new Grand-Craft brand boat owners.[357]

By 1990, the company was employing sixteen craftsmen and producing about six boats annually, averaging six hundred man hours per boat, or about nine months. That same year, Outboard Marine Corporation (OMC), then owner of the Chris-Craft name, contacted Chris Smith and asked him to select a classic Chris-Craft boat design and build twenty-four boats for the company. Smith turned the order over to Grand-Craft, which contracted with OMC to build twenty-four triple-cockpit boats. Between 1990 and 1991, Grand Craft completed fifteen of that model before sales dried up and the two parties decided to stop production. Grand Craft would later design its own twenty-four-foot triple-cockpit model for consumers.[358]

By 1995, the company, like most of the luxury boat industry, was benefiting from booming sales and had fully recovered from the 1991 10 percent tax on luxury items imposed in the United States on material goods, including boats and yachts, over $100,000.[359] That year, Grand-Craft offered consumers five sport runabouts (twenty-one to twenty-eight feet), five classic runabouts (twenty-two to thirty-six feet) and three hardtop commuters (thirty, thirty-six and forty-two feet) per year. Prices ranged from $35,000 (twenty-one-foot Sport Runabout) to $250,000 (forty-two-foot Commuter). Unlike the early Grand-Crafts, which were heavily influenced by older Chris-Craft designs, the Sligh-era designs were largely created by Dick Sligh, with input from Chris Smith. The sport boat line incorporated style characteristics seen in wooden boats from the 1950s and 1960s. The classic boat line was inspired by the styles seen in boats from the 1920s and 1930s. That year, Sligh predicted that the company would earn $1 million in gross sales, with hopes of tripling gross sales in two years.[360] In a 1996 magazine interview for *Lakeland Boating*, Sligh stated that the company had been building about twenty boats per year with fifteen employees and planned to add more personnel and increase production to fifty to seventy-five boats per year.[361]

In 2001, Sligh reported employing fifteen employees and averaging eighteen of the twenty-four-foot Runabout model per year, each taking about ten months to build, with a cost of $124,000 to $165,000, depending on special equipment and custom touches. The forty-eight-foot cabin cruisers started at $1 million.[362]

By the time the Slighs had sold the business in May 2005, they had annual sales of $2.5 million, had increased the space of the company to twenty-two thousand square feet, were employing sixteen employees, were making a boat every three to four months and had built custom boats for customers like actors Tim Allen and George Clooney, actress-singer Jennifer Lopez, professional basketball star Joe Dumars, furniture and interior designer Barbara Barry and singers Merle Haggard and Kid Rock. Dick Sligh reported that he and Marti had personally sold, designed, oversaw construction, delivered each boat and made sure that each owner felt very comfortable with their new Grand-Craft before leaving. His marketing plan consisted of word-of-mouth sales from current owners and advertising in a handful of luxury magazines, like the *Robb Report*. Under this system, the company produced eighteen boats during its best sales year.[363]

In May 2005, Chicago-based TMB Industries purchased the company. Tim Masek, who held a 25 percent share in the company and had a passion for wooden boats, was appointed president of the company and incorporated it as Grand-Craft Acquisitions, LLC. The Slighs stayed on to direct the design, production and marketing aspects of the corporation. From the onset, Masek reported that he wanted to double the size of the business within twelve to eighteen months by doubling the number of employees and utilizing more of the company floor space, now made up of several older wooden buildings, for production of thirty boats per year, ranging in size from twenty-four to forty feet. In August 2006, the company reported sales of $2.6 million, with hopes of expanding production to about thirty boats per year.[364]

In December 2006, Masek resigned from TMB Industries and announced in January 2007 that he had purchased Grand-Craft Acquisitions, LLC, outright, becoming the sole owner of the newly named Grand Craft Boat Company. Sale of the company became official in October 2007.[365] The forty-three-year-old Masek's background was running foundries, stamping companies and buying and selling more than thirty-five companies across the United States. He found the position a welcome change from operating and owning smokestack manufacturing businesses that were underperforming, according to an April 16, 2007 *MiBiz* article. In that same article, he was quoted as saying that "owning the company gave him a chance to be involved with an exclusive high-end product and a very stable workforce of twenty-five people who have a passion for what they're doing." At that time, the company offered seventeen standard boat models, ranging in size from twenty to forty feet, for prices between $65,000 and $1.5 million.[366]

Soon, the company's boats were appearing in prestigious money magazines like the *Robb Report, Stratos, Yachts International* and *Millionaire Yachts* and being sighted around the world.[367] In the May 28, 2007 edition of the *Grand Rapids Business Journal*, Masek stated that orders were twelve months out for their standard models, starting at $69,000, and that they were on course to produce between twenty-five and thirty boats for the year. Masek even predicted that a new manufacturing facility might be needed by 2009, the company's thirtieth anniversary, to produce thirty of a line of thirty-foot boats. It appeared that his goals of immediate and significant growth through more capital, and the creation of a full-time marketing department, headed by Corey Koopmans, built on the tested personal sales approach and new ideas, were working for the company, then reported to be worth $10 million.[368]

In the spring of 2008, the State of Michigan featured two Grand-Craft boats in the foreground and Big Red Lighthouse in the background on the cover of its state road map.[369] The company also joined forces with Cincinnati, Ohio–based Antique Boat Center to produce and market a new Contemporary Classic runabout, styled very much like the 1946–49 model years' twenty-foot Chris-Craft Custom. The Antique Boat Center held the exclusive rights to market this boat model.[370] Later that same year, the company announced the introduction of the revolutionary Volvo-Penta IPS drive system on its larger models, including the new forty-two-foot express cruiser. It was the first wooden boat manufacturer to incorporate this system, which allowed greater maneuverability of the boat by pulling the boat through the water (tractor drive) versus pushing it with more traditional approaches.[371] That same year, the company took another nontraditional approach, marketing its boats to exclusive housing associations and hotels, like those at the Reserve at Lake Keowee, located near Greenville, South Carolina, and Hotel Janelle, located in Harbor Springs, Michigan. At both facilities, owners and visitors could use a Grand-Craft during their stay, as well as work with a sales representative to purchase a Grand-Craft of their very own.[372]

In September 2008, the company launched its own interactive website that allowed potential customers access to information and images of the company's complete line of boats. Customers of the company, spending between $80,000 and $1.6 million for a boat, were given even more access, as they were able to login and actually watch their boat being built by a team of twenty-eight master craftsmen via webcam, as well as get images of the boat building process, right up to the eighteenth and last coat of varnish, with e-mail and phone access to a customer representative if they had a question about their boat or wanted to plan a plant visit. With a projected build time of eight to fifteen months, customers had ample opportunity to check out their custom-built boat.

The company also launched and made available through its website the LUXE Brokerage, an affiliated company that specialized in selling new and pre-owned Grand-Craft boats.[373] Later that month, Corey Koopmans left his vice-president of sales and marketing position at Grand-Craft to take a job with Vicem Yachts USA and was replaced by James Sheely. The company also was represented in Europe by Switzerland-based Rolf Geter of GMC Marine Limited.[374] By all appearances, the company's future looked bright, even though Sheely remarked in an October newspaper article that inquiries were down from past years. On December 23, workers were sent home with no expectations to return. In February, a small group was called back to finish a boat but was then laid off, according to Dick Sligh in a 2009 *Holland Sentinel* article.

In February 2009, Dick Sligh retired as president from the company that he and his wife had grown from very little to world class in reputation. By June, the *Holland Sentinel* reported that the company was "beached" and up for sale by owner Tim Masek, whose LinkedIn profile detailed his departure from the company in April 2009. Inside the factory, about eight boats remained unfinished, 50 to 75 percent completed. The closure left twenty employees jobless.[375] Masek ended his ownership of the business in 2009, with no sale to a new buyer. The factory was then idle, except for the removal of unfinished boats and equipment after sale by creditors.

The Grand-Craft brand did not die with the 2009 closure of the Grand Craft Boat Company. In 2010, Jeff Cavanaugh, president of Anchorage Marine Service, purchased two unfinished boats and the assets of the company, still owned by the Slighs after the uncompleted sale to TMB

Industries and Masek. Cavanaugh renamed it Grand Craft Boats, LLC, and moved it to Anchorage Marine Boatyard, located at 1821 Ottawa Beach Road in Holland. By 2012, Cavanaugh and his crew of craftsmen, made up of many former Grand Craft Boat Company employees, had completed those two boats and two more new boats for customers.[376] By October 2013, the company was made up of a crew of ten to nineteen building a few fine wooden custom boats per year from five standard models to custom orders, ranging from $100,000 to $1.6 million. Customers at the time included Michigan governor Rick Snyder, as well owners contracting for refinishing and restoring of older Grand-Craft boats.[377] In 2016, the company announced the expansion to a ten-thousand-square-foot space in one of the former Chris-Craft company buildings located at 60 Chris-Craft Way, built in 1986 for fiberglass production. There, Grand Craft built its new twenty-five-foot Super Sport powerboat and introduced it at fall boat shows for a price of $279,000. The company reported that its staff of ten built about five boats per year, each one taking seven to eighteen months to build, ranging in size from twenty to forty-two feet and priced from $120,000 to $1.5 million.[378]

POWER PLAY BOAT COMPANY/POWERQUEST BOATS

Power Play Boat Company was founded in 1983 by Kevin Hirdes, a former insurance agent, and aspiring boat builder Todd Kamps with the construction of an eighteen-foot fiberglass boat. Hirdes and Kamps became acquainted in 1978 while water skiing together on Hess Lake, Newaygo County, Michigan. In January 1983, while Kamps was working for Grand Haven, Michigan–based Cary Marine Inc. making fifty-foot powerboats, he rented an eighteen-foot boat mold from the owners of the defunct Grand Rapids–based Baron Boat Company, Bruce and Dave Diephouse, for $1,500 and set to work making a personal eighteen-foot sport boat in the Cary Marine plant. Later that spring, Hirdes learned of Kamps's project and joined him to help with the finishing touches. In June, the boat was complete, and after much testing, the two were impressed with how well the boat performed and purchased the mold for $5,000.[379] The two formed the idea of building more of the ruggedly built sport boat with sleek lines—the Cadillac of boats, according to an early company brochure. H and K Boating Industries (later Power Play Boat Company) was formally founded on August 16, 1983. The new company was founded on a front porch between two good friends with a start-up capital of $7,000. The more familiar Power Play boat brand was derived from the name Kamps had placed on the first boat he had made with Hirdes in Grand Haven.

Soon after the two purchased the mold, some basic tools and materials, they started building the first Power Play Boat Company boat, which was based on the Baron hull with modifications to the cockpit to make it more appealing to consumers. That boat became the XLT-185 (which was derived from the letter *X*; Kevin's middle name, *Lee*, and the names of his wife, *Linda* Hirdes, and *Todd* Kamps; and the length of the boat) and was built in a space rented for $200 per month from Bill Mouw, owner of GPM Industries, located at 429 West Twenty-Third Street. With little working capital, the two rented gel coat and resin guns from Mouw during the evening, who used the same tools to make hot tubs and pools for his company during the day.[380]

With the first boat built and more planned, Hirdes and Kamps decided to look for a larger space to rent but could not find a landlord willing to rent to them. So, the two young boat builders, with family and friends, funded the $35,000 purchase of a few acres of property at 2385 112th Street and building materials for a 2,600-square-foot pole building in the fall of 1983.[381] A few months later, in early 1984, Hirdes and Kamps took their first boat to a boat show in Chicago. When they left the show, they had one deposit check in their hands for their low-priced $14,000 boat, but the buyer backed out of the order by the time the two arrived back in Holland. Next, they showed their boat in Grand Rapids, where two customers placed orders, but they canceled their orders too. The two then decided that a dealer network was needed to effectively sell their boats. Their first dealer, Holland-based Anchorage Yacht Sales, sold their first boat to Len Miller, a friend of Hirdes's. In total, the dealer sold the first six boats, worth $200,000 in sales, as well as taking a few boats into inventory, which was the total for their first model year. The second dealer, based in Detroit, was Jefferson Beach Marina.

In 1985, the small company, sometimes using family members to help build boats, hired its first employee of many, Larry Brouwer, a former Tiara Yachts employee. Eventually, Tom Lampen from Chris-Craft and expert gel coat applier Jim Wright (sometimes known as "Mr. X" for his quality work) from Tiara Yachts approached Hirdes and Kamps about wanting to work for Power Play, which made the company products even better. That year, the growing company made and sold forty boats to consumers.[382]

In 1986, it made and sold 90 boats. Additions to the plant were made in 1986 and 1987, totaling thirty-five thousand square feet. The next year,

125 boats were sold through thirty-three dealers throughout the Midwest and eastern seaboard. In 1986, the company introduced the very popular 230 Conquest model, which incorporated all the features found in the XLT-185 but in a bigger boat.[383] Through the late 1980s, the company's well-defined strategy of creating a quality product for the discerning buyer and maintaining a very controlled growth, all while resisting major growth toward becoming an "all things to all people" boat company, served it well. That strategy allowed it to add only one new boat model each year, which included two sizes, eighteen and twenty-three feet, powered by stern-drive V6 and V8 engines, ranging in price from $28,000 to $40,000.[384]

In May 1988, Kamps sold his interest in the company to Hirdes and new partner John Spoelhof, then president of the locally owned Prince Corporation. This ownership change allowed the young company to gain immense business experience. Kamps remained at the company, where he was a spokesperson at boat shows, in addition to playing a key role in the manufacturing process and quality assurance—assuring that the quality he and Hirdes originally intended when the company was founded was still being upheld and implemented in the manufacturing process on a daily basis. Kamps left the company in 1993 to pursue a career in commercial and industrial real estate.[385] In August of that year, company owners announced plans to add another thirteen thousand square feet to the existing plant to house their very skilled, forty-employee staff, which Hirdes referred to as "Team Power Play." They also announced plans to design, with the help of the talented designers Ed Wennersten and Doug Wilson, and build a twenty-two-foot model, the very contemporary and aggressively styled 222 Spectra XL and later the Bow Rider version, for their still small brand.[386]

The last sixth months of that year ended with the company's expanding line of boats being highlighted as prizes on thirty episodes of the popular game show *Wheel of Fortune*. Wennersten and Wilson finished out the 1980s by designing the twenty-nine-foot offshore model, the 290 Enticer F/X. This model was copied into many of the models that followed and firmly placed the company among the best in the business.[387] Even at that early stage in the company's history, Hirdes was able to pinpoint their quick success to dedication to quality through details such as high-tech manufacturing techniques, hand-laminated fiberglass hulls, hand-stitched upholstery and so on. That attention to detail earned them the unofficial title of the "BMW" or "Mercedes Benz" of the sport boat industry by dealers.[388]

In 1992, the company sold the name Power Play Boat Company to Florida-based powerboat manufacturer Powerplay Powerboats Inc.

to avoid a copyright conflict and mounting court costs. The company renamed the company PowerQuest Boats Inc., which was derived from the first name of the previous brand name, Power, and the last five letters of their popular 230 Conquest model. While the name changed, company philosophy remained the same, as the company continued to make high-quality boats ranging from twenty-two to twenty-seven feet. That year, the company introduced the 270 Laser, which was heavily influenced by the 290 Enticer F/X, bringing the company's offerings up to eight models and five different lengths. The next year, the company offered seven different lengths and introduced the 208 Viate XL, 208 Viate BR (bowrider), 257 Legend XL and 257 Legend BR. The 237 Stryker XL and 237 Stryker BR were added to the line in 1994. Many of the exotic-sounding model names came from discussions had at holiday gatherings of friends and family when a new model was being designed.[389]

In 1995, the plant was expanded for the sixth time to include another fifteen thousand square feet to the already twenty-thousand-square-foot manufacturing facility footprint, in addition to the separate ten-thousand-square-foot building that housed company offices, upholstery and wood-framing departments and raw material storeroom. The expansion allowed more room for both lamination and final assembly, which in turn increased the company's efficiency and output.[390] That year, it projected $9 million in sales from its ten models of boats, ranging in size from twenty-two to thirty-eight feet, including the newly introduced 380 Avenger and 340 Vyper models, with the help of engineering concepts from local firms like Bonnette Design, which were instrumental in the development of the thirty-eight- and thirty-four-foot boats. The forty to sixty employees built boats that ranged in price from $33,000 to $300,000 and were sold around the world including the Netherlands, Great Britain, Switzerland, Belgium, Spain, Italy, Greece, Japan and Thailand. The following year, the company introduced three new models: the 220 Targa SX, the 220 Targa SLS and the 240 Antera SX. The 1998 model year saw the introduction of the 22 Raizor and the performance stepped-bottom 280 Silencer.[391] That same year, the company announced the purchase of property adjacent to the existing plant, with plans for more manufacturing space for more lines and models for its ninety employees to build.[392]

PowerQuest was purchased by an investment group led by Jack Moll and Rick Koster in May 2001. While tough for Hirdes personally, he wanted to venture into new business opportunities, and selling the business was necessary to do so. The company, under Koster and Moll, continued making boats from 2001 to September 2005, when it was shuttered after losing $3.5 million over a four-year period.[393]

In January 2007, the idle company's assets were purchased by Muskegon boat builder Phil Hall's Coastal Performance Marine, LLC, from PQ Holdings. Hall, forty-seven years old at the time, had spent eighteen years in the boat building business making mainly high-end, high-performance, offshore powerboats like AeroTec. Hall, now calling the company PQ Marine Holdings Inc., put his plan in action when he hired back ten former employees, like fifteen-year company veteran Carlos Beltran, with hopes of producing new boats, like the $250,000 thirty-eight-foot Avenger model, in July of that year. He also planned on producing and selling a new model, the $500,000 forty-foot 400 SC Sport Cruiser through a sixteen-member U.S. and three-member international dealer network. The company limped along until ending production in July 2009, after Hall and others had invested an undisclosed amount of money in redesigning the boats but ultimately never selling any.[394]

In December 2011, the company's assets (now owned by a secured creditor)—which included the now thirteen-acre site and buildings, a full line of boat molds, motors, partially completed boats, parts inventory, paint booths, pickup trucks and heavy equipment—were sold off via an online auction site owned by Miedema Auctioneering & Appraisals (Orbitbid.com).[395]

In March 2012, most the buildings of the defunct company were demolished to make way for new buildings for the Muskegon, Michigan–based Harbor Steel and Supply Corporation. One remaining thirty-thousand-foot building was renovated for the new company.[396]

Westease Yacht Service Inc./New Holland Marine Group

New Holland Marine Group was originally founded as Westease Yacht Service Inc. in 1985 by Jon Easley and Will Westrate as a mobile repair business servicing and modifying high-performance racing sailboats. The partners took advantage of a truth little known outside the world of racing: owners of racing boats will go to any length to gain an edge in speed or maneuverability. The business grew over the years and occupied some of Holland's historic boat building facilities, like the former Campbell Boat Company/Beacon Boat Company/South Shore Marine site, located at 1691

Weastease crew rolling a new hull, 1998. *New Holland Marine Group Inc. Collection.*

South Shore Drive, from 1985 to 1990; the former Chris-Craft Corporation factory from 1990 to 2001; and the Broward Yachts location in Saugatuck from 2001 to 2007.[397]

In 1989, the company built updated production molds of the International 110 sailboat. Over the years, new boats were built and delivered to clients from the Midwest to the East Coast. Construction of the International 110 boats continues today. The company also built the three-fourth-ton racer *Footloose* designed by Graham & Schalageter in 1985.[398]

During the 1990s, the firm diversified into other industries, utilizing its core competencies in composite fabrication. Some notable projects included building composite doors for military containers, sign façades used on national landmarks and experimental carbon fiber fifth wheels for the trucking industry. The company has been a parts supplier for a number of other organizations, including Tiara Yachts and Melges Boat Works in Zenda, Wisconsin. The company built production tooling for Offshore Spars in Chesterfield, Michigan, a company that supports the mega yacht industry in Europe. The company built numerous custom racing sailboats for clients and notable naval architects, successfully competing in events worldwide. These boats included the MORC thirty-foot Racer *Zoo II* designed by Alan Andrews Yacht Design in 1991; the MORC thirty-foot

Racer *Zoo III* designed by Nelson/Marek Yacht Design in 1993, which went on to win the MORC Internationals by the largest margin ever and won the 1994 Canada's Cup as *Champion Eagle*; the MORC thirty-foot Racer *Invincible* designed by Nelson/Marek Yacht Design in 1994, which was built to compete in the 1994 Canada's Cup and went on to win MORC Internationals in 1996; and the IMS forty-three-foot Racer *Vim* designed by Nelson/Marek Yacht Design in 1996, which won the IMS World Championship in Newport, Rhode Island, in 2000. The company also built the SHY (Short Handed Yacht) forty-foot *C-Spray* for single-handed sailing in 1998, which won numerous events and set records.[399]

The company has completed numerous refits, modifications and optimizations over the years and continues this type of work today. Projects include modifications on the Great Lakes 70s *Nitemare*, *Denali*, *Stripes*, *Holua*, *Equation* and *Colt 45*. The company has also refitted the OD48 class boats for the National Sailing League. Numerous modifications have also been made to the well-known yachts *Il Mostro*, *Windquest*, *Vincitore*, *Heartbreaker*, *Natalie J.*, *Lucky*, *Whisper* and *Imedi*. In addition to big boat optimizations, the firm has a constant stream of Etchells and other one-designs flowing through the shop seasonally.[400]

In 2007, the company name changed to New Holland Marine Group Inc. In recent years, it has expanded its reach globally with clients in England and France, as well as serving the 2016 Rio Olympics, where the company supported the Nacra 17 Gulari / Chaffee Olympic campaign handling all the boat building and performance development projects.[401]

The Future

The volatile economy and trend toward conglomerates in the pleasure boating industry during the last fifty years has worked against the development of new boat building companies in Holland. The only firms to take on the tough times and succeed include custom makers of replica wooden powerboats and fiberglass boats powered by large engines, styled in bright colors and custom-made fast-sailing designs. The trend toward building one boat at a time in a small building until a level of production requiring a factory was achieved worked well until the market required higher production and craftsmen desired higher wages and better benefits. Those companies were also purchased by larger companies and eventually closed due to the latest recession. Today, only three boat building companies call Holland home and are building boats for custom orders or in very small numbers to satisfy consumer demand. From more than fifty companies, there are now only three, but all three are nationally recognized for their craft. Holland is proud to claim them. More than 175 years have passed since the wooden ship *A.C. Mitchell* first floated out onto Black Lake. In the interim, the community of Holland has grown by leaps and bounds, and so did its boat building industry, which successfully accommodated the demand for commercial ships, military craft and pleasure boats. Only time and creativity will tell if Holland will return to its former heights of boat production.

NOTES

Chapter 1

1. Weston Farmer, "Those Wonderful Naptha Launches," *Yachting*, July 1973, 38–39, 88.

2. "A New Industry," *Grand Rapids Evening Leader*, December 2, 1892, 1.

3. Advertisement, *Daily Resorter*, September 1, 1894.

4. "Grand Rapids Gossip," *Michigan Tradesman*, December 12, 1894, 5.

5. Advertisement, *Summertime–Ottawa Beach*, Macatawa Park brochure, circa 1898, 20, Holland Promotional Materials Collection (H05-1575.2), JAH.

6. Ibid.

7. Paul Towne, "The Naphtha Engine," *Gas Engine Magazine* (October/November 1991).

8. "Goes to Holland," *Grand Rapids Evening Press*, November 12, 1900, 1.

9. "Secured by Holland," *Detroit Free Press*, November 13, 1900, 3.

10. Ibid.

11. "Thirty-Eight Foot Launch," *The Rudder*, January 1902, 18; Wolverine Motor Works brochure, 1902, 48, Geoffrey Reynolds Collection (H00-1389), JAH (hereafter noted as (H00-1389)).

12. *Ottawa County Times*, October 6, 1901, 8.

13. Ibid., January 25, 1901, 8; "For Arctic Seas," *Grand Rapids Evening Press*, March 8, 1901; "Another Industry, Western Machine Tool Works Will Locate Here," *Holland City News*, July 19, 1901, 1.

14. Advertisement, *The Rudder*, July 1901, 20; *Grand Rapids City Directory*, 1902, 1,247.

15. "Localisms," *Ottawa County Times*, May 6, 1904, 8.

16. "Will Move East," *Grand Rapids Evening Press*, December 11, 1905, 2; "Local News," *Holland City News*, December 14, 1905, 4.

17. "City and Vicinity," *Holland City News*, November 9, 1905, 1; ibid., June 16, 1905, 1.

18. "Additional Local," *Holland City News*, December 21, 1905, 8.

19. "Local News," *Holland City News*, March 8, 1906, 1.

20. Ibid.

21. "City and Vicinity," *Holland City News*, January 10, 1907, 1, 4; *Michigan Investor* 5, no. 14 (January 5, 1907): 3.

22. "City and Vicinity," *Holland City News*, December 20, 1906, 1.

23. Ibid.; *Michigan Investor* 5, no. 16 (January 19, 1907): 11.

24. *Michigan Investor* 5, no. 10 (December 8, 1906): 18.

25. "Local," *Holland City News*, January 3, 1907, 8; "Boat Works to Begin Operations at Once," *Holland City News*, January 10, 1907, 4.

26. *Michigan Investor* 6, no. 37 (June 20, 1908): 17; "Bradshaw Saw Chicago as a Prairie in 1847," *Holland City News*, July 23, 1925, 1.

27. *Standard Atlas of Ottawa County, Michigan*, 1912, 25.

28. "Factory of Holland Launch and Engine Co. Partly Destroyed," *Holland City News*, July 2, 1914, 6.

29. *Insurance Maps of Holland, Ottawa County, Michigan*, October 1916.

30. Scrapbook Two, Lois Jesiek Kayes Collection (H03-1505), JAH (hereafter noted as (H03-1505)).

31. Ibid.

32. Ibid.

33. Ibid.

34. Ibid.

35. Ibid.

36. Ibid.

37. International 110 Fleet 46, "International 110 Fleet 46 History," http://international110fleet46history.blogspot.com/2008/06/about-110-specifications-designer.html; "Rebuilding an International 110," *Epoxy Works*, no. 23 (Spring 2006): 10–11.

38. Scrapbook Two (H03-1505).

Chapter 2

39. "Holland Will Have Steel Boat Plant," *Holland City News*, June 14, 1934, 1; *Polk's Holland (Ottawa County) City Directory*, 1936, 363.

40. City of Portland, Maine Death Certificate, no. D 673; brochure, "New Gil-Boat Price List, January 1, 1938," Cherry Overway Collection.

41. "Holland Will Have Steel Boat Plant," *Holland City News*, June 14, 1934, 1.

42. "Gil-Boat Co. to Start within Thirty Days," *Holland City News*, November 22, 1934, 1.

43. "Boat Concern Is Ready to Start," *Grand Rapids Press*, November 23, 1934, 8.

44. "Pressed Steel Boats Made without Ribs, Stem or Stern Posts," *Iron Age*, August 1, 1935, 23; "Ribless, Welded Pressed Steel Boats," *Sheet Metal Worker*, September 1935, 417–18.

45. "Steel Outboard Boats," *Motor Boating*, January 1937, 361.

46. Harrison M. Reed Jr. to Captain M.L. Gilbert, undated, Gil-Boat Company, Customers, 1935–42 (H00-1389).

47. *Michigan Manufacturer and Financial Record* 57, no. 12 (March 21, 1936): 70.

48. Ibid., no. 23 (March 28, 1936): 13; "Gil-Boat Company Stock Certificate, May 6, 1936," Business & Industry Collection, HMARL.

49. *Michigan Manufacturer and Financial Record* 57, no. 17 (April 25, 1936): 45.

50. *Polk's Holland (Ottawa County) City Directory*, 1936, 86, 110.

51. *Michigan Manufacturer and Financial Record* 59, no. 5 (January 30, 1937): 6.

52. Ibid., no. 13 (March 27, 1937): 14.

53. "Specifications of Outboard Boats," *Motor Boating*, January 1937, 314; "Wisconsin Ruling on Boat Explained," *Holland Evening Sentinel*, August 30, 1938, 7.

54. "Seven-Screw Unsinkable Ship Hits Eighty-Mile Clip at Sea," *Popular Mechanics*, August 1939, 187; E.J. Jenkins, "The New Alloy of Magnesium," *Iron Age*, July 22, 1929, 193–94.

55. "Says Clipper Test Is Success," *Holland City News*, July 20, 1939, 4.

56. *Polk's Holland (Ottawa County) City Directory*, 1940, 85.

57. "Asks Receiver at Local Firm," *Holland City News*, July 3, 1940, 3.

58. "Two Claims Against Gil-Boat Company Are Heard," *Holland Evening Sentinel*, March 29, 1941, 1.

59. "Gil-Boat Concern of Holland Sold," *Holland City News*, April 23, 1942, 1.

60. Robert J. Gomez, "Something New in Freighters, *Shipping Digest*, January 20, 1942, 1–2, Clippings, Beacon Boat Company (H00-1389).

61. "Letter from Captain M.L. Gilbert to President Franklin D. Roosevelt, January 28, 1942," Gil-Boat Company, Customers, 1935–42 (H00-1389).

62. Mark Leroy Gilbert, City of Portland, Maine Death Certificate, no. D 673, May 20, 1943.

63. Oral interview with Ethel Sincock, February 12, 2003 (H00-1389).

64. Kenneth Hoatson Campbell necrology file, University of Michigan Alumni Files, Bentley Historical Library, the University of Michigan; Calumet-Laurium section, unidentified Michigan newspaper, May 1954, Campbell Boat Company, Holland Business File, JAH.

65. "Kenneth Campbell Succumbs After Extended Illness," *Holland Evening Sentinel*, May 18, 1954, 1; "Boat Building Plant on Lake Macatawa," *Holland City News*, August 26, 1937, 1.

66. "Boat Building Plant on Lake Macatawa," *Holland City News*, August 26, 1937, 1.

67. Oral interview with Ethel Sincock.

68. "Boat Building Plant on Lake Macatawa," *Holland City News*, August 26, 1937, 1.

69. "Additions at Two Boat Firms Near Completion," unidentified newspaper, 1939, Campbell Boat Company, Local Business File, JAH.

70. Ibid.

71. Advertisement, *The Rudder*, May 1940, 118; advertisement, *The Rudder*, September 1940, 49; e-mail correspondence with Mike Pearson and Geoffrey D. Reynolds, March 29, 2017, Campbell Boat Company, owners (H00-1389).

Chapter 3

72. "Start Work on Holland Plant of Chris-Craft," *Holland City News*, August 3, 1939, 1.

73. "Continue Work on Boat Plant," *Holland City News*, August 10, 1939, 7.

74. "Boat Company Founder Dead," *Holland City News*, September 14, 1939, 7.

75. "Work on Boats at Chris-Craft to Start Soon," *Holland City News*, November 16, 1939, 1.

76. Ibid.; "Five Classes of Boats in Chris-Craft 1940 Fleet," *The Rudder*, January 1940, 70–71.

77. "Chris-Craft to Turn Out 1940 Models at Holland Branch," *Motor Boating*, January 1940, 242.

78. "Chris-Crafts Sold at New York Show," *Motor Boating*, February 1940, 87.

79. "When Chris-Craft Plant Shipped Its First Boat," *Holland Evening Sentinel*, February 6, 1940, 3.

80. "Chris-Craft Gets Army Order," *The Rudder*, November 1940, 71.

81. "Motor Boats for Defense," *Motor Boating*, March 1941, 60, 113.

82. "Chris Craft Will Receive Navy E," *Holland City News*, May 28, 1942, 1.

83. "Three Navy 'E's for Excellence in Production," *The Rudder*, July 1942, 64; "Triple Ceremony Honors Chris-Craft," *The Rudder*, August 1942, 37.

84. "Three Navy 'E's for Excellence in Production," *The Rudder*, July 1942, 64; "Chris-Craft Military Boats," *The Rudder*, October 1942, 55; "Contact with Chris-Craft," *The Rudder*, October 1942, 64; "Walkout Extended to Three Boats Plants," *Holland City News*, August 27, 1944, 1.

85. Larry McDonough, "The Holland Plant: The First Satellite—Part 2," *Brass Bell* (Winter 1994): 3.

86. Jeff Rogers, "Chris Smith: Heir to a Legend," *Waterline* (Summer 2000): 20–26.

87. "Walkout Extended to Three Boats Plants," *Holland City News*, August 27, 1944, 1.

88. Ibid.

89. "Walkout at Boat Company Ends," *Holland City News*, May 4, 1944, 7.

90. "Chris-Craft Out on Sympathy Strike," *Holland City News*, August 30, 1945, 1; "Strike Is Ended at Chris-Craft," *Holland City News*, November 1, 1945, 1.

91. "Anecdotes and Reminiscences on Chris Smith's Tour of the Chris-Craft Holland Plant," *Classic Boating* (September/October 2006): 23.

92. "Letter from Jesiek Brothers Ship Yard to Commander Wynekoop, Bureau of Ships, Navy Building, Washington, D.C., April 17, 1942" (H03-1505).

93. "Letter from Bill Jesiek to Lois Jesiek Kayes, December 3, 1996" (H03-1505).

94. "Sub-Chaser Goes to New Orleans," *Holland City News*, January 14, 1943, 1; "Impressive Rites Mark Launching of Naval Vessel," *Holland City News*, December 3, 1942, 1.

95. "Impressive Rites Mark Launching of Naval Vessel," *Holland City News*, December 3, 1942, 1.

96. "Letter from Victory Shipbuilding Company to Chief of the Bureau of Ships, Navy Department, Washington, D.C., October 36, 1942" (H03-1505).

97. "Second Sub Chaser Is Launched," *Holland City News*, January 21, 1943, 1.

98. "Launch USN Harbor Tug, First of a Series, Here," *Holland City News*, June 28, 1943, 2.

99. Ibid.

100. Photograph and caption, *The Rudder*, January 1941, 138; advertisement, *The Rudder*, December 1942, 56.

101. Oral interview with Ethel Sincock.

102. "New Boat Firm Is Formed Here," *Holland City News*, December 31, 1942, 1.

Chapter 4

103. "Face-Lifting for a Sprightly Old Gal," *Lakeland Yachting*, January 1947, 23–24; "Marinas of the Lakes," *Lakeland Yachting*, June 1947, 13.

104. Laverne Berry, "From Bait Shop to Modern Marina," *The Boating Industry*, March 1951, 29–30, 98.

105. Ibid.

106. Oral interview with Ethel Sincock.

107. "Scuttlebutt-Holland," *Lakeland Yachting*, January 1946, 16; "Tahoma Cuts Channel for Launching of Tug," *Holland City News*, January 3, 1946, 1.

108. "Campbell Building Malabar Jr.," *Lakeland Yachting*, September 1946, 19.

109. Interview with Robert Bennett, February 21, 2003 (H00-1389).

110. "West Michigan," *Lakeland Yachting*, September 1950, 30.

111. "Stock Boat Builders Selling Through Dealers," *The Boating Industry*, January 10, 1951, 54; advertisement, *Lakeland Yachting*, January 1947, 36; advertisement, *Lakeland Yachting*, April 1949, 41; "Local Boat Company Launches New Craft," *Holland Evening Sentinel*, September 19, 1947, 1; "Campbell Boat Firm Is Leased to Milwaukee Man," *Holland City News*, July 16, 1953, 7.

112. Advertisement, *Lakeland Yachting*, September 1948, 30; "Campbell Holiday," *Lakeland Yachting*, January 1949, 42.

113. "Motor Boating's Specifications—1949 Sail, Motor-Sailers and Auxiliaries," *Motor Boating*, January 1949, 194.

114. "Local Boat Company Launches New Craft," *Holland Evening Sentinel*, September 19, 1947, 1; "What's New in Power & Sail," *Lakeland Yachting*, November 1950, 18–19.

115. "Kenneth Campbell Succumbs After Extended Illness," *Holland City News*, May 20, 1954, 1.

116. "1953 Boat Builders," *Motor Boating*, January 1953, 234.

117. "Kenneth Campbell Succumbs After Extended Illness," *Holland City News*, May 20, 1954, 1.

118. "Pleasure Boats Being Built by Beacon Boat Co.," *Holland City News*, July 5, 1956, 1.

119. "Kenneth Campbell Succumbs After Extended Illness," *Holland City News*, May 20, 1954, 1; funeral program of Kenneth H. Campbell, May 19, 1954 (H00-1389).

120. "Mildred M. Campbell," *Holland Evening Sentinel*, August 28, 1996, A6.

121. "Contract Signed at Chris Craft," *Holland City News*, May 1, 1947, 3.

122. Advertisement, *Lakeland Yachting*, January 1949, 37.

123. Interview with Robert Bennett; "Chris-Craft Corp. Buys Roamer Boat Co.," *Lakeland Boating*, April 1955, 44.

124. "Welded Steel Cruiser by J. Murray Watts," *The Rudder*, July 1948, 82.

125. J. Murray Watts, "Welding for Small Steel Boats," *The Rudder*, July 1941, 14–16; Wallace R. Wirths, "Winter Overhauling of Steel Cruisers," *Motor Boating*, February 1947, 124–25.

126. "Builds Boats and Sells Cruisers," *The Boating Industry*, April 1948, 83.

127. *Polk's Holland (Ottawa County) City Directory*, 1947–48, 148.

128. "Builds Boats and Sells Cruisers," *The Boating Industry*, April 1948, 83.

129. Advertisement, *Lakeland Yachting*, April 1948, 10; advertisement, *The Rudder*, June 1948, 80; "Roamer Boat Co. Expands," *Lakeland Yachting*, September 1948, 23.

130. "New Torch Lake Boat Line," *Lakeland Yachting*, March 1948, 23; "Roamer Boat in Passenger Service," *Lakeland Yachting*, July 1948, 28.

131. *Michigan Manufacturer and Financial Record* 82, no. 1 (July 1948): 32; phone interview with Roland E. Ladewig in Murrayville, Georgia, February 2, 2013, Roamer Boat Company (H00-1389).

132. "Roamer Boat Company Brochure, 1949," Cruiser and Tug Brochures, Roamer Boat Company Collection (T94-1368), HMARL.

133. "Roamer Building 38-Footer," *Yachting*, January 1953, 303.

134. "Roamer Boat Co. Gets Okay to Build Warehouse," *Holland City News*, November 19, 1953, 2.

135. Interview with Robert Bennett.

136. "Chris-Craft Corp. Buys Roamer Boat Co.," *Lakeland Yachting*, April 1955, 44.

137. "Chris-Craft Buys Roamer Boat Co.," *Holland City News*, March 31, 1955, 1; "Chris-Craft Corp. Buys Roamer Boat Co.," *Lakeland Boating*, April 1955, 44.

138. "Bay Haven Marina," *Lakeland Yachting*, June 1955, 69; "Robert R. Linn," May 30, 1994, Herrick District Library Obituary File.

139. Interview with Phyllis Pelgrim White, November 19, 2001 (H00-1389).

140. Articles of Incorporation for the Mac-Bay Boat Company, May 1, 1948, Minute Book, 1948–62, Mac Bay Boat Company Collection (H11-1773), JAH (hereafter noted as (H11-1773)).

141. "New Industry Makes Boats; Unique Design," *Holland Evening Sentinel*, June 30, 1948, 6; phone interview with Fred A. Kaunitz, Bay City, Michigan, January 10, 2005, Mac Bay Boat Company (H00-1389); *Polk's Holland and Zeeland (Ottawa County, Mich.) City Directory*, 1947–48, 128.

142. Advertisement, *Lakeland Yachting*, January 1949, 11.

143. Interview with Phyllis Watkins Cox, May 12, 2003 (H00-1389).

144. "Watkins Building Playboy," *Yachting*, January 1948, 150.

145. "New Industry Makes Boats; Unique Design," *Holland City News*, July 1, 1948, 1.

146. Advertisement, *Yachting*, February 1949, 109.

147. "Watkins Showing Grayboy Runabouts," *Lakeland Yachting*, January 1949, 33.

148. Advertisement, *Lakeland Yachting*, January 1949, 11.

149. Stock Holder Meeting, July 15, 1949, Minute Book, 1948–62 (H11-1773).

150. Ibid., August 3, 1949, Minute Book, 1948–62 (H11-1773).

151. "President of Victor E. Watkins Co. Dies in Auto Accident on August 7," *The Boating Industry*, August 15, 1949, 36.

152. "Victor E. Watkins Dies in Car Crash," *Holland Evening Sentinel*, August 8, 1949, 1; Certificate of Death for Victor Edwin Watkins, Emmet County, Michigan, August 7, 1949.

153. "Bowman Mfrs., Inc. Has a New Craft to Tempt This Year's Marine Buyers," *The Boating Industry*, March 10, 1958, 170.

154. Certificate of Death for Lester R. Kaunitz, County of Washtenaw, State of Michigan, April 26, 1976.

155. Interview with William de Boer, September 30, 2002 (H00-1389).

156. "Fire Damages Building," *Holland City News*, November 13, 1952, 5; "Heinz Purchases Bay View Factory," *Holland City News*, July 1, 1954, 1.

157. "Mac Bay Molded Ply Boats," *Yachting*, January 1953, 258; "New Inboards," *Lakeland Yachting*, February 1953, 38.

158. Interview with William de Boer; Board of Directors Meeting, December 20, 1954, Minute Book, 1948–62 (H11-1773).

159. Board of Directors Meeting, February 19, 1955, Minute Book, 1948–62 (H11-1773).

160. Shareholders Meeting and Board of Directors Meeting, July 5, 1955, Minute Book, 1948–62 (H11-1773).

161. Advertisement, *The Boating Industry*, August 1956, 187.

162. "Chris-Craft Corp. Buys Roamer Boat Co.," *Lakeland Boating*, April 1955, 44.

163. "Mac Bay Boat Company to Move to Muskegon," *The Boating Industry*, April 1956, 253.

164. Interview with Clifford G. Dobben, June 5, 2001 (H00-1389).

Chapter 5

165. Geoffrey D. Reynolds, "Plastic Fantastic: The Fiberglass Boatbuilding Industry in Holland, Michigan," in *Michigan Modern*, 199–206.

166. Ibid.

167. Ibid.

168. "Jesiek Bros. Shipyard Founder Dies," *The Boating Industry*, August 15, 1956, 66.

169. "West Michigan," *Lakeland Yachting*, February 1956, 118; advertisements, *Lakeland Boating*, April 1957, June 1959, 54; Scharff, *One-Design Class Sailboat Handbook*, 123–24; "Pleasure Boats Being Built by Beacon Boat Co.," *Holland City News*, July 5, 1956, 1; "Michigan 110s," *Lakeland Yachting*, September 1955, 54.

170. "H.F. Jesiek Is Reported Drowned," *Holland City News*, August 8, 1958, 1; "Examiner Rules Death Accidental," *Holland City News*, August 14, 1958, 5.

171. Advertisements, *Lakeland Boating*, June 1959, 46; May 1960, 50; May 1961, 52.

172. "The Oldest Dealerships," *The Boating Industry*, July 1976, 45.

173. "Celebration of the Life of William Jesiek, August 17, 1918 to August 13, 2012," funeral program (H00-1389).

174. "Chris-Craft Corporation Plans Factory Addition: New Addition Will Add 200 Persons to Local Plant," *Holland Evening Sentinel*, July 17, 1950, 1.

175. Ibid.

176. McDonough, "Holland Plant," 4.

177. Joseph A. Loftus, "White House Ends All Wage Control, Many Price Curbs," *New York Times*, February 7, 1953.

178. "New Chris-Craft Contract Signed," *Holland City News*, March 19, 1953, 3.

179. "Violence Erupts at Local Plant," *Holland City News*, March 25, 1954, 1.

180. "Negotiations to End Chris Craft Strike Scheduled," *Holland City News*, March 25, 1954, 1.

181. "Chris-Craft Corp. Withdraws Offers," *Holland City News*, April 8, 1954, 7.

182. "Chris-Craft Lays Off 14 Office Personnel," *Holland City News*, April 8, 1954, 6; "Chris-Craft Corp. Withdraws Offers," *Holland City News*, April 8, 1954, 7.

183. "Strike Settled as Both Sides Come Together," *Holland City News*, April 22, 1954, 7.

184. "Chris-Craft Office Damaged" and "Direct Lightning Hit Razes Barn North of Holland," *Holland City News*, May 26, 1955, 1; "Chris-Craft Office Building Damaged by Fire," *Holland City News*, May 26, 1955, 4.

185. McDonough, "Holland Plant"; "Announce Top Appointments in Chris-Craft Organization," *The Boating Industry*, March 15, 1955, 160.

186. Reynolds, "Plastic Fantastic."

187. "Correspondence to All Lake-N-Sea Boat Dealers and Chris-Craft Department Heads from Wayne Pickell, Vice President, June 27, 1957," Chris-Craft Archives, MS00005.

188. "Chris-Craft in Fiberglass Boat Field," *Motor Boating*, August 1957, 48.

189. "Boatbuilding Empires Sold: NAFI Corp. Pays 40 Million for Chris-Craft; Brunswick-Balken-Collender Buys Owens," *Motor Boating*, April 1960, 128, 130, 132.

190. "Chris-Craft Buys Roamer Boat Co.," *Holland City News*, March 31, 1955, 1; "City Offers to Purchase Roamer Land," *Holland City News*, October 23, 1958, 1; McDonough, "Holland Plant."

191. Advertisement, *Motor Boating*, May 1955, 99; "Roamer," *Motor Boating*, January 1956, 118.

192. "Chris-Craft Will Build New Factory on Lakewood Blvd.," *Holland City News*, May 10, 1956, 1; "Mike Potter Appointed," *Lakeland Boating*, April 1960, 30.

193. "Roamer Steel Boats Will Occupy New Holland, Michigan Plant Late This Year," *The Boating Industry*, June 1956, 156; "Roamer Boat Builds New Plant," *Lakeland Boating*, July 1956, 41; "Fall Meeting at Holland," *The Megaphone*, September 1957, Clippings, Roamer Yachts Division of

Chris-Craft Corporation Collection (H05-1550.6) (hereafter noted as (H05-1550.6)).

194. "Harry H. Coll Has Received the Appointment as President of the Chris-Craft Corp.," *The Boating Industry*, January 1959, 645; photograph and caption, *Lakeland Boating*, May 1959, 48.

195. "Roamer Boat Co.," *The Boating Industry*, January 10, 1959, 198.

196. "Campbell Boat Firm Is Leased to Milwaukee Man," *Holland City News*, July 16, 1953, 7; *Lakeland Boating*, May 1959, 57; *Oracle*, 1928, 78.

197. Advertisement, *Lakeland Yachting*, February 1954, 54, 75; "Motor Boating's Specifications—1954 Cruisers and Express Cruisers," *Motor Boating*, January 1954, 238, 244, 260; "Local Boat Firm Gets $365,521 Navy Contract," *Holland Evening Sentinel*, March 2, 1954, 1; "U.S. Defense Contracts Awarded Michigan Firms U.S. Navy 40' Utility Boat—Beacon Boat Co., Holland—$372,752," *Michigan Manufacturer and Financial Record* 93, no. 4 (April 1954): 32.

198. Photograph and caption, *Holland City News*, December 9, 1954, 4; photograph and caption, *Lakeland Yachting*, March 1955, 50.

199. "Scattered Damage Reported as Wind Whips Lake Water," *Holland City News*, March 24, 1955, 3; advertisement, *Lakeland Yachting*, August 1955, 30.

200. "Boats of the United States Navy," *The Boating Industry*, May 15, 1956, 46.

201. Oral interview with Ethel Sincock.

202. Advertisement, *Lakeland Yachting*, October 1955, 37; advertisement, *Lakeland Yachting*, November 1955, 49; advertisement, *Lakeland Yachting*, December 1955, 34; advertisement, *Lakeland Yachting*, January 1956, 44.

203. Advertisement, *Lakeland Yachting*, February 1956, 108; "Pleasure Boats Being Built by Beacon Boat Co.," *Holland City News*, July 5, 1956, 1.

204. Advertisement, *Lakeland Yachting*, March 1957, 64; Scharff, *One-Design Class Sailboat Handbook*, 90–99, 124–27.

205. "West Michigan," *Lakeland Boating*, December 1958, 38.

206. Advertisement, *Lakeland Boating*, March 1959, 62.

207. "West Michigan," *Lakeland Boating*, May 1959, 56–57; *Polk's Holland and Zeeland (Ottawa County, Mich.) City Directory*, 1960, 16, 59; correspondence with Jim Gretzky, January 18, 2017, Beacon Boat Company (H00-1389).

208. Social Security Administration, *Social Security Death Index, Master File*, certificate no. 85-17331.

209. Interview with Jason Petroelje, September 6, 2000 (H00-1389).

210. Ibid.

211. Ibid.

212. Ibid.

213. "Jason Petroelje," *Holland Evening Sentinel*, April 29, 2015.

214. Interview with Clyde Poll, January 23, 2001 (H00-1389); *The Boomerang*, 1953, 27; *Polk's Holland and Zeeland (Ottawa County, Mich.) City Directory*, 1960, 59, 259.

215. Interview with Clyde Poll.

216. Ibid.

217. Ibid.

218. Ibid.

219. Ibid.; *Polk's Holland and Zeeland (Ottawa County, Mich.) City Directory*, 1960, 59.

220. "Slickcraft Co. Purchased by New York Firm," *Holland Evening Sentinel*, September 26, 1969, 2.

221. Dave Mull, "Leon Slikkers," *Lakeland Boating*, August 2001, 32–35.

222. Interview with Leon Slikkers, September 18, 2001 (H00-1389).

223. Interview with Merle Cook, August 20, 2002 (H00-1389).

224. Interview with Leon Slikkers, September 18, 2001.

225. Ibid.

226. Ibid.

227. Ibid.

228. "G.E. Bonnette, Controller, Slickcraft Boat Company to Mr. Walter J. Sullivan III, Boats Unlimited Corp, September 8, 1967," Dealers Correspondence, 1962–66 (H00-1389).

229. Ibid.; "Slickcraft Co. Purchased by New York Firm," *Holland Evening Sentinel*, September 26, 1969, 2.

230. Brochures, 1957, Slick Craft Boat Company (H05-1564).

231. Interview with Leon Slikkers, September 18, 2001; brochures 1957 and 1958, Slick Craft Boat Company (H05-1564). This company name also appears in some sources as Camfield Fibre Glass Plastics Inc.

Chapter 6

232. "Boatbuilding Empires Sold: NAFI Corp. Pays 40 Million for Chris-Craft; Brunswick-Balken-Collender Buys Owens," *Motor Boating*, April 1960, 128, 130, 132; "NAFI Votes to Buy the Chris-Craft Corp.," *The Boating Industry*, May 1960, 283.

233. McDonough, "Holland Plant"; "Pace for the 60s," *Motor Boating*, November 1960, 42–43, 70, 140; "Holland Division of Chris-Craft Elects Fredericks Vice President," *The Boating Industry*, December 1960, 162.

234. Rodengen, *Legend of Chris-Craft*, 201; "Anecdotes and Reminiscences on Chris Smith's Tour," 21.

235. "New Chris-Craft Fiberglass Cruiser," *Yachting*, January 1964, 322.

236. McDonough, "Holland Plant"; "A Man, a Company and Boats," *Motor Boating*, November 1961, 38–39, 78–80, 82; "How's Business," *The Boating Industry*, December 1964, 12.

237. "Negotiators Hold Meeting," *Holland City News*, May 12, 1966, 1.

238. McDonough, "Holland Plant."

239. Photograph and caption, *Lakeland Boating*, May 1959, 48; "George Smith Gets 30-Year Award," *Holland City News*, June 20, 1963, 7.

240. Roamer Yachts Division brochure, 1962 (H05-1550.6).

241. "Chris-Craft's Roamer Yacht Division," *Yachting*, January 1962, 162; "Roamer Yachts Div.," *The Boating Industry*, January 1965, 373.

242. Martin Luray, "The Case for Aluminum Boats," *The Rudder*, 34–38, 62, 65–67, 72.

243. Rodengen, *Legend of Chris-Craft*, 201.

244. "Slickcraft Co. Purchased by New York Firm," *Holland Evening Sentinel*, September 26, 1969, 2; interview with David Slikkers, February 28, 2005 (H00-1389).

245. "Slick Craft Boat Company Brochure and Price List, 1960," Slick Craft Boat Company (H05-1564).

246. Ibid.

247. "Slickcraft Co. Purchased by New York Firm," *Holland Evening Sentinel*, September 26, 1969, 2; "Boat Firm Builds Plant, Warehouse," *Holland City News*, July 8, 1965, 4; "Boat Name Directory," *The Boating Industry*, November 1964, 334, 336; phone interview with George Dalman, Holland, Michigan, June 8, 2017, Slick Craft Boat Company Collection (H00-1389).

248. "Boat Firm Builds Plant, Warehouse," *Holland City News*, July 8, 1965, 4.

249. "Special Notice to All Slick Craft Dealers correspondence from Leon R. Slikkers, Sales Manager, August 8, 1962," Slick Craft Boat Company, Dealers Correspondence, 1962–66 (H00-1389); sales invoice from Robert B. Hamilton Company to Morehouse Boat Company, March 20, [1962], Dealers Correspondence, 1962–66, Slick Craft Boat Company (H00-1389).

250. "SlickCraft Direct Dealer Agreement, Slick Craft Boat Company, Holland, Michigan, Morehouse Boat Co., Inc., March 25, 1963," Dealers Correspondence, 1962–66, Slick Craft Boat Company (H00-1389).

251. Interview with Ed Wennersten, January 16, 2002 (H00-1389).

252. Interview with Leon Slikkers, September 18, 2001.

253. "Slick Craft Boat Company Brochure and Price List, 1962," Slick Craft Boat Company (H05-1564).

254. Interview with Robert Egan, January 30, 2002 (H00-1389); "Slick Craft Boat Co.," *The Boating Industry*, January 1965, 180.

255. "Slick Craft Boat Company brochure, 1969," Slick Craft Boat Company (H05-1564); "Grew Boat Company brochure, 1969," Slick Craft Boat Company (H00-1389).

256. Interview with Leon Slikkers, September 18, 2001; Grew Boats Brochure, 1969, Slick Craft Boat Company (H00-1389); Slick Craft Boat Company Brochure, 1969, Slick Craft Boat Company (H05-1564).

257. Obituary, "Dennis G. Slikkers, 84," *Holland Evening Sentinel*, June 19, 2003, A6.

258. "Slick Craft Boat Company Correspondence to All Slick Craft Dealers, June 23, 1964," Dealers Correspondence, 1962–66, Slick Craft Boat Company (H00-1389).

259. "Slickcraft Co. Purchased by New York Firm," *Holland Evening Sentinel*, September 26, 1969, 2; "G.E. Bonnette, Controller, Slickcraft Boat Company, to Mr. Walter J. Sullivan III."

260. "G.E. Bonnette, Controller, Slickcraft Boat Company, to Mr. Walter J. Sullivan III."

261. "Boat Firm Builds Plant, Warehouse," *Holland City News*, July 8, 1965, 4.

262. Interview with Leon Slikkers and Thomas Holmes, February 19, 2013 (H00-1389); Thomas Holmes, "Century Cheetah by Slikkers," *Thoroughbred Newsletter* (Spring 2013): 10–11.

263. "Addition Slated for Slick Craft," *Holland Evening Sentinel*, April 4, 1968, 11; "Slickcraft Co. Purchased by New York Firm," *Holland Evening Sentinel*, September 26, 1969, 2.

264. "Slickcraft Purchases Property," *Holland City News*, September 12, 1968, 10.

265. "Vande Vusse Is Named to Post," *Holland City News*, November 21, 1968, 5; e-mail correspondence with Gerry and Robert VandeVusse and Geoffrey Reynolds, March 20, 2017 (H00-1389).

266. "Be Our Guest, Open House, Monday Evening, May 26, 7 to 9," *Holland Evening Sentinel*, May 23, 1969, 9; "Slickcraft Co. Purchased by New York Firm," *Holland Evening Sentinel*, September 26, 1969, 2.

267. "AMF, Inc. v. Sleekcraft Boats, 599 F.2d 341 (9th Circuit 1979)," retrieved on November 24, 2005, from http://cyber.law.harvard.edu/metaschool/fisher/domain/tmcases/amf.htm; "Slickcraft," Trademark

Electronic Search System (Tess), retrieved from http://tess2.uspto.gov/bin/showfield?f=doc&state=tlbfdr.2.3.

268. "Slickcraft Co. Purchased by New York Firm," *Holland Evening Sentinel*, September 26, 1969, 2.

269. Also listed as Michigan Fiberglass Plastics Inc. according to Meyering's circa 1969 résumé, Lawrence V. Meyering Collection (H02-1436), JAH (hereafter noted as (H02-1436)).

270. The University of Wisconsin Seventy-Fifth Commencement Register, June 28, 1928; Northwestern University Commencement Program, June 15, 1931.

271. Meyering's circa 1969 résumé (H02-1436); *A Look Behind the Scenes at Camfield*, brochure (Grand Haven, MI: circa 1962) (H02-1436).

272. Interview with Henry Kort, April 26, 2002 (H00-1389).

273. Interview with John Schutten, September 27, 2002 (H00-1389).

274. "Parsons Suspends 1961 Production of Its Lake 'n Sea Line of Boats," *The Boating Industry*, December 1960, 170.

275. Lake 'n Sea Division, Folder 8, Box 90, John T. Parsons Collection (MS1987-016), Special Collections, Virginia Tech University.

276. Interview with Henry Kort; "Michigan Porpoise Sailboat Available," *The Boating Industry*, June 1962, 158.

277. *The Beachcomber*, brochure, undated, L.V.M. Associates Inc. (H02-1436).

278. Interview with Henry Kort; correspondence with June Vos, August 21, 2002, Correspondence, Michigan Fiberglass Company (H00-1389).

279. Interview with Henry Kort; correspondence with June Vos; advertisement, *The Boating Industry*, September 1963, 190; "Molded Products Co.," *The Boating Industry*, January 1964, 256.

280. Social Security Applications and Claims, 1936—007, Social Security Administration; "Lawrence Valentine Meyering," *Grand Rapids Press*, October 12, 1993, provided by Grand Rapids Public Library.

Chapter 7

281. McDonough, "Holland Plant," 6.

282. "Russell J. Fredericks Succumbs at Age 65," *Holland Evening Sentinel*, January 16, 1979, 3.

283. McDonough, "Holland Plant," 6; "Anecdotes and Reminiscences on Chris Smith's Tour," 18–23.

284. Pete McDonald, "After the Fall," *Boating*, October 2002, 129–31.

285. "An Old Name with a New Twist," *Boating*, January 1988, 59–60, 62, 64.

286. Mike Lozon, "Chris-Craft Woes Tied to Old Plant," *Holland Evening Sentinel*, January 20, 1989, A10; "Chris-Craft Produces Final Boat; Plant Closes," *Holland Evening Sentinel*, January 28, 1989, B8.

287. Mike Lozon, "Chris-Craft Transformation: Small Companies Work Out of Plant Where Boats Were Once Manufactured," *Holland Evening Sentinel*, January 25, 1990, B7; Mike Lozon, "A Building with a Future— Former Chris-Craft Plant Provides Environment for Success," *Holland Evening Sentinel*, October 16, 1994, C1, C8; Mark Sanchez, "A Home for the Little Guys," *Holland Evening Sentinel*, July 18, 1999, B1, B3.

288. McDonough, "Holland Plant," 7.

289. "Slickcraft Co. Purchased by New York Firm," *Holland Evening Sentinel*, September 26, 1969, 2.

290. "Slickcraft Starts Third Expansion," *Holland City News*, November 16, 1972, 7; interview with David Slikkers, February 22, 2002 (H00-1389).

291. "Camarota Named Slickcraft Head," *Holland City News*, November 29, 1973, 1.

292. "AMF Agrees to Offer by Jacobs of $24 a Share," *New York Times*, June 15, 1985, retrieved March 25, 2017; "Details for Manufacturer Identification Code SLK," retrieved on March 3, 2007, from www.uscgboating.org/recall/mic_detail.aspx?id=SLK.

293. "Camarota Named Slickcraft Head," *Holland City News*, 1; Dave Mull, "Leon Slikkers," *Lakeland Boating*, August 2001, 32–35.

294. Myron Kukla, "S2 Yachts Celebrates 30th Year, but Start Came Years Earlier," June 27, 2004, *Grand Rapids Press*, June 28, 2004.

295. Interview with Leon Slikkers, April 8, 2002 (H00-1389).

296. "A Historical Perspective," Tiara Yachts 2000 Dealer Manual, 1, Tiara Yachts (H05-1564); interview with David Slikkers, February 22, 2002.

297. Robert Egan; interview with Richard Thede, January 30, 2002 (H00-1389).

298. Interview with David Slikkers, February 28, 2002 (H00-1389).

299. Ibid.; "Historical Perspective," 1.

300. "Historical Perspective," 2.

301. "New Corporations. Lovecraft Boat Company," *Michigan Manufacturer and Financial Record* 125, no. 1 (January 1970): 34; interview with Yvonne Love, January 3, 2002 (H00-1389).

302. "Lovecraft's Fiberglass Puppy Love Is 10' Catamaran Paddlewheeler," *Lakeland Boating*, July 1970, 36; Lovecraft Boat Company brochure, undated, Lovecraft Boat Company Collection (H05-1583.5), JAH;

Lovecraft Boat Company sales correspondence, undated, Lovecraft Boat Company Collection (H05-1583.5), JAH.

303. Interview with Yvonne Love.

304. Ibid.

305. Ibid.

306. Ibid.

307. Interview with Kenneth Voss, January 21, 2002 (H00-1389).

308. Interview with Yvonne Love.

309. Ibid.

310. Ibid.

311. Ibid.

312. Ibid.

313. Ruskcraft Company letterhead, undated, Ruskraft Company Collection (H05-1583.6), JAH.

314. Interview with Forest Homkes by Geoffrey D. Reynolds, March 11, 2002 (H00-1389).

315. Interview with Yvonne Love.

Chapter 8

316. Interview with David Slikkers, February 28, 2002.

317. "S2/Tiara Yachts 8 Days from Local Debut," *News Tribune*, July 3, 1983, B10.

318. Interview with Thomas Slikkers, January 14, 2014 (H00-1389).

319. "Historical Perspective," 2; interview with Thomas Slikkers.

320. "Historical Perspective," 2.

321. Ibid.

322. Massie, "S2 Yachts, Inc.," *The Holland Area*, 107.

323. Dave Mull, "Leon Slikkers," *Lakeland Boating*, August 2001, 32–35.

324. "Historical Perspective," 2.

325. Ibid.

326. Ibid.

327. Ibid.

328. Sallie Gaines, "Ship Shapers: Building Production Boats a Hands-On Experience," *Chicago Tribune*, May 30, 1993, Section 17, 1, 7.

329. "Historical Perspective," 2.

330. Gaines, "Ship Shapers"; Christine Jann, "Making Waves," *Grand Rapids Press*, September 14, 1993, L3.

331. "Historical Perspective," 2.
332. Interview with Thomas Slikkers.
333. "Historical Perspective," 2.
334. Ibid.
335. Ibid.
336. Ibid.
337. Mark Sanchez, "Sailing into Boating History: Leon Slikkers Inducted into the National Marine Industry Hall of Fame," *Holland Evening Sentinel*, September 19, 1999.
338. "Historical Perspective," 2; Sanchez, "Sailing into Boating History."
339. "S2 Yachts Changes Leadership," *Holland Evening Sentinel*, August 25, 2001.
340. Joe Skorupa, "Boating in the Blood," *Marine CEO*, January 2003, 1–4.
341. Kukla, "S2 Yachts Celebrates 30th Year"; "S2 Yachts: More than 50 Years, and Still Going Strong," *Marine Business Journal*, August 2008, 28–30.
342. Myron Kukla, "S-2 Yachts Expands Plant in Holland," *Grand Rapids Press*, August 24, 2005.
343. "S2 Yachts Pursues Diversification," *Business Review Western Michigan* (June 25–July 1, 2009): 6, 9.
344. Andréa Goodell, "Energetx Scores $2 Million in Clean Energy Tax Credits," *Holland Evening Sentinel*, January 9, 2010; Nathan Hurst, "Stimulus Funds Patch Up Michigan Roads, Schools," *Detroit News*, April 21, 2010; Ben Beversluis, "Energy Excellence Designation, $7 Million, Given to Energetx Wind Turbine Development in Holland," *Holland Evening Sentinel*, April 29, 2010.
345. Stephen Kloosterman, "S2 Yachts, Energetx Moving Ahead, Building Yachts for Netherlands Firm," *Holland Evening Sentinel*, September 22, 2011.
346. Rick Barrett, "Marquis Yachts Settles Lawsuit Against VanDutch Marine," *Milwaukee Journal Sentinel*, May 11, 2005.
347. Interview with Thomas Slikkers; Chris Landry, "Talkin' Boats with Tom Slikkers President and CEO of S2 Yachts," *Soundings*, March 30, 2015.
348. Ray Anthony, "Sophisticated Ladies: Elegant Classic Designs Wedded to New Technology," *Boating World*, August/September 1995, 31–37.
349. Larkin, *Grand and Glorious*, 55; Anthony, "Sophisticated Ladies."
350. Larkin, *Grand and Glorious*.
351. Interview with Richard Sligh, September 10, 2001 (H00-1389); Myron Kukla, "At Grand-Craft, Wood Still Floats Their Boat," *Holland Evening Sentinel*, April 5, 2001.

352. Amber Veverka, "Magical Mahogany," *Grand Rapids Press*, August 24, 1995, A1; Bob Pearson, "Watershed in the Woodshop," *Lakeland Boating*, September 1996, 67–70.

353. Brochures, Grand Craft Boats, LLC, Collection (H06-1466.2), JAH (hereafter noted as (H06-1466.2)).

354. Laurie Anderson, "Movie Star Knocks at Holland's Door for Custom Boats," *Holland Evening Sentinel*, July 9, 1990, A1, A3.

355. Interview with Richard Sligh.

356. "Grand Craft Unveils Boat," *Holland Evening Sentinel*, August 1, 1987, A12.

357. *Grand-Craft Newsletter* (Fall 1987–February/March 2006), Newsletters, 1987–2006 (H06-1466.2).

358. Anderson, "Movie Star Knocks at Holland's Door"; Kukla, "At Grand-Craft, Wood Still Floats Their Boat."

359. "Good Riddance to the Luxury Tax," *Wall Street Journal*, January 6, 2003, retrieved May 5, 2017.

360. Amber Veverka, "Magical Mahogany: Even Robert Redford Owns a Grand Craft Corp. Boat," *Holland Evening Sentinel*, August 21, 1995, A1, A6.

361. Pearson, "Watershed in the Woodshop," 67–70.

362. Kukla, "At Grand-Craft, Wood Still Floats Their Boat."

363. Patrick Revere, "Boat Maker Hopes to Make a Bigger Splash After Sale," *Holland Evening Sentinel*, May 15, 2005, D3; Myron Kukla, "Mahogany Vessels Turn Heads Worldwide," *Grand Rapids Press*, August 6, 2006, 1N–2N.

364. Kukla, "Mahogany Vessels Turn Heads Worldwide."

365. "Boat Maker Has New Ownership," *Holland Evening Sentinel*, November 14, 2007, B9; Nancy Crawley, "New Skipper Guides Boat-Building Tradition," *Grand Rapids Press*, October 14, 2007, F1, F4.

366. Karen Gentry, "Boatbuilders Creating Smooth Economic Wake," *MiBiz*, April 16, 2007, retrieved May 20, 2009.

367. Michael Schulze, "Grand-Craft, First Loves," *Robb Report*, April 2007, 171–76; Crawley, "New Skipper Guides Boat-Building Tradition."

368. Daniel Schoonmaker, "Grand-Craft Picks Up Speed," *Grand Rapids Business Journal*, May 28, 2007, retrieved May 5, 2017.

369. Greg Chandler, "Lakeshore Boat Maker Part of Michigan Map's Theme," *Grand Rapids Press*, March 5, 2008, retrieved May 5, 2017.

370. "If You Can't Find 'Em Used," *Brass Bell* (Summer 2008): 7.

371. "Grand-Craft Announces Production of New 42-Foot Express Cruiser with Revolutionary Volvo-Penta IPS Drives," September 4, 2008, Clippings, 1981–2010 (H06-1466.2).

372. "Grand Craft Featured at the Reserve at Lake Keowee," October 31, 2008, Clippings, 1981–2010 (H06-1466.2); "Grand-Craft and Hotel Janelle Announce Strategic Partnership," Clippings, 1981–2010 (H06-1466.2).

373. Thomas Jackson, "Grand Again," *Forbes Life*, June 2008, 78–81; "Grand-Craft Interactive Web Site," September 16, 2008, Clippings, 1981–2010 (H06-1466.2).

374. "Vicem Yachts USA Welcomes New Broker Corey Koopmans," October 2, 2008, SuperYachtTimes.com, retrieved June 18, 2014; Grand Craft Corporation website, retrieved February 20, 2009.

375. Jeremy Gonsior, "Classic Boat Maker Beached," *Holland Evening Sentinel*, June 13, 2009, A1–A2; "Tim Masek," LinkedIn, retrieved May 20, 2009.

376. Stephen Kloosterman, "Holland's By-Gone Wooden Boat Era Still an Inspiration," *Holland Evening Sentinel*, August 6, 2012, retrieved August 6, 2012.

377. Alex Shabad, "Made in Michigan: Grand Craft Mahogany Boats," *WZZM13*, retrieved June 3, 2014; Shandra Martinez, "This New $279K Boat Is Why Grand-Craft Opened 2nd Plant in Holland," July 14, 2016, MLive.com, retrieved July 28, 2016.

378. Justine McGuire, "Holland's Grand Craft Boats to Manufacture in Former Chris Craft Building," *Holland Evening Sentinel*, July 12, 2016, retrieved July 12, 2016; Martinez, "This New $279K Boat."

379. Interview with Todd Kamps, February 17, 2004 (H00-1389).

380. Ibid.

381. "The PowerQuest Story," History, circa 1999, PowerQuest Boats (H03-1520), JAH; Mike Lozon, "PowerQuest Boats Floats Yet Another Building Expansion," *Holland Evening Sentinel*, March 2, 1995, B7; interview with Todd Kamps.

382. Interview with Kevin Hirdes, December 1, 2003 (H00-1389); interview with Todd Kamps.

383. "PowerQuest Story"; interview with Kevin Hirdes.

384. Jim Harger, "Success Means Fun for Boat Builder," *Grand Rapids Press*, August 14, 1988; "PowerQuest Story"; interview with Kevin Hirdes.

385. Interview with Kevin Hirdes.

386. "PowerQuest Story"; advertisement, *Lakeland Boating*, July 1989, 114; Lozon, "PowerQuest Boats," B7.

387. "PowerQuest Story"; interview with Kevin Hirdes.

388. Harger, "Success Means Fun for Boat Builder."

389. "PowerQuest Story"; interview with Kevin Hirdes.

390. Lozon, "PowerQuest Boats."

391. Ibid.; "PowerQuest Story."

392. Mary Ann Sabo, "Boat Bonanza: West Michigan Craftsman Happily Bailing Under a Flood of Orders," *Grand Rapids Press*, August 8, 1999, F1, F4; interview with Kevin Hirdes.

393. Interview with Kevin Hirdes; "PowerQuest Boats," *NAFTA Register*, retrieved April 28, 2017.

394. Myron Kukla, "Boat Company Is Afloat Again," *Grand Rapids Press*, undated but circa July 2009; Myron Kukla, "PowerQuest's Use of Green Products Saluted," *Grand Rapids Press*, December 9, 2007; Shandra Martinez, "Holland Speedboat Maker PowerQuest Boats Hits Auction Block," *Grand Rapids Press*, December 3, 2011; interview with Kevin Hirdes.

395. Martinez, "Holland Speedboat Maker PowerQuest"; Stephen Kloosterman, "Auctions Kick Off for Assets of Holland Boat Builder PowerQuest," *Holland Evening Sentinel*, December 6, 2011, retrieved May 9, 2017.

396. Stephen Kloosterman, "Former PowerQuest Site Prepped for Harbor Steel Relocation," *Holland Evening Sentinel*, March 20, 2012, retrieved April 28, 2017.

397. "Westease Yacht Service-New Holland Marine Group History," 2017, New Holland Marine Group Collection (H17-1960), JAH.

398. Ibid.

399. Ibid.

400. Ibid.

401. Ibid.

BIBLIOGRAPHY

Archival Collections

Business & Industry Collection. Holland Museum Archives and Research Library, Holland, Michigan (HMARL).

Chris-Craft Archives collection (MS00005). The Mariner's Museum Library, Newport News, Virginia.

Geoffrey D. Reynolds Collection (H00-1389). Joint Archives of Holland, Hope College, Holland, Michigan (JAH).

Grand Craft Boats, LLC, Collection (H06-1466.2). Joint Archives of Holland, Hope College, Holland, Michigan (JAH).

Grand Rapids Public Library, Grand Rapids, Michigan.

Holland Business File. Joint Archives of Holland, Hope College, Holland, Michigan (JAH).

Holland Promotional Materials Collection (H05-1575.2). Joint Archives of Holland, Hope College, Holland, Michigan (JAH).

John T. Parsons Collection (MS1987-016). Special Collections, University Libraries, Virginia Tech University, Blacksburg, Virginia.

Lawrence V. Meyering Collection (H02-1436). Joint Archives of Holland, Hope College, Holland, Michigan (JAH).

Lois Jesiek Kayes Collection (H03-1505). Joint Archives of Holland, Hope College, Holland, Michigan (JAH).

Lovecraft Boat Company Collection (H05-1583.5). Joint Archives of Holland, Hope College, Holland, Michigan (JAH).

Mac Bay Boat Company Collection (H11-1773). Joint Archives of Holland, Hope College, Holland, Michigan (JAH).

New Holland Marine Group Collection (H17-1960). Joint Archives of Holland, Hope College, Holland, Michigan (JAH).

Roamer Boat Company Collection (T94-1368). Holland Museum Archives and Research Library, Holland, Michigan (HMARL).

Roamer Yachts Division of Chris-Craft Corporation Collection (H05-1550.6). Joint Archives of Holland, Hope College, Holland, Michigan (JAH).

Ruskraft Company Collection (H05-1583.6). Joint Archives of Holland, Hope College, Holland, Michigan. (JAH).

S2 Yachts Inc. Collection (H05-1564). Joint Archives of Holland, Hope College, Holland, Michigan. (JAH).

Slickcraft Boat Division of AMF Collection (H05-1564.5). Joint Archives of Holland, Hope College, Holland, Michigan (JAH).

University of Michigan Alumni Files. Bentley Historical Library, University of Michigan, Ann Arbor, Michigan.

Books

Arnold, Amy L., and Brian D. Conway, eds. *Michigan Modern: Design that Shaped America*. Layton, UT: Gibbs-Smith, 2016.

The Boomerang. Yearbook. Holland, MI: Holland High School, 1953.

Conrad, Jerry. *Chris-Craft: The Essential Guide*. Newport News, VA: Mariners' Museum, 2002.

Larkin, Larry. *Grand and Glorious: Classic Boats of Lake Geneva*. Lake Geneva, WI: Sealark Publications, 2002.

Massie, Larry B. *The Holland Area (Michigan) Warm Friends and Wooden Shoes: An Illustrated History*. Northridge, CA: Windsor Publications Inc.—History Books Division, 1988.

Oracle. Yearbook. Milwaukee, WI: Bay View High School, 1928.

Peters, Scott. *Making Waves: Michigan's Boat-Building Industry, 1865–2000*. Ann Arbor: University of Michigan Press, 2015.

Rodengen, Jeffrey L. *The Legend of Chris-Craft*. 3rd ed. Fort Lauderdale, FL: Write Stuff Syndicate Inc., 1998.

Scharff, Robert. *One-Design Class Sailboat Handbook*. New York: G.P. Putnam's Sons, 1961.

Directories

Grand Rapids City Directory. Detroit, MI: R.L. Polk & Company, 1901.

Holland City Directory. Marion, IN: Inter-State Directory Company, 1906.

Polk's Holland and Zeeland (Ottawa County, Mich.) City Directory. Detroit, MI: R.L. Polk & Company.

Polk's Holland (Ottawa County, MI) City Directory, 1940. Detroit, MI: R.L. Polk & Company, 1940.

Maps

Insurance Maps of Holland, Ottawa County, Michigan. New York: Sanborn Map Company, October 1916.

Standard Atlas of Ottawa County, Michigan. Chicago: Geo. A. Ogle & Company, 1912.

Newspapers

Chicago Tribune. Chicago: Tronc Inc.

Daily Resorter. Petoskey, Michigan.

Detroit Free Press. Detroit, Michigan.

Detroit News. Detroit, MI: Gannett.

Grand Rapids Evening Leader. Grand Rapids, Michigan.

Grand Rapids Evening Press/Grand Rapids Press. Grand Rapids, Michigan.

Holland City News. Holland, Michigan.

Holland Evening Sentinel/Holland Daily Sentinel/Holland Sentinel. Holland, Michigan.

News Tribune. Fort Pierce/Port St. Lucie, Florida.

New York Times. New York City, New York.

Ottawa County Times. Holland, Michigan.

Wall Street Journal. New York: Dow Jones and Company.

Periodicals, Television Stations and Websites

Boating. New York: Bonnier Corporation.

The Boating Industry. New York: National Trades Publications.

Brass Bell. Oxford, OH: Chris-Craft Antique Boat Club.

Business Review Western Michigan. Grand Rapids, MI: MLive Media Group.

Classic Boating. Oconomowoc, Wisconsin.

Epoxy Works. Bay City, MI: Gougeon Brothers Inc.

Forbes Life. Jersey City, NJ: Forbes Media, LLC.

Gas Engine Magazine. Topeka, KS: Ogden Publications Inc.

Grand Rapids Business Journal. Grand Rapids, MI: Gemini Publications.

Iron Age. New York: Iron Age Publishing Company.

Lakeland Yachting/Lakeland Boating. Evanston, IL: Lakeland Boating/O'Meara-Brown Publications.

Marine Business Journal. Fort Lauderdale, Florida.

Marine CEO. Hilton Head Island, SC: Marine Design Resource Alliance.

MiBiz. Grand Rapids, Michigan.

Michigan Investor. Detroit, MI: Michigan Bankers Association.

Michigan Manufacturer and Financial Record. Detroit, MI: Manufacturer Publishing Company.

Michigan Tradesman. Grand Rapids, MI: Tradesman Company.

Motor Boat. New York: Motor Boat Publications Inc.

Motor Boating. New York: Hearst Corporation.

NADAGuides. N.p.: National Appraisal Guides Inc.

NAFTA Register. Marlton, NJ: Global Contact.

Outboard. Tallahassee, FL: Outboard Publishing Company Inc.

Peninsular Club Magazine. Grand Rapids, MI: Peninsular Club.

Popular Mechanics. Chicago: H.H. Windsor.

Power Boating. New York: Bonnier Corporation.

Robb Report. New York: Robb Report Media, LLC.

Rudder. Clayton, NY: Antique & Classic Boat Society.

The Rudder. New York: Rudder Publishing Company.

Sheet Metal Worker. Tarrytown, NY: Edwin A. Scott Publishing Corporation.

Ship's Lamp. South Haven: Michigan Maritime Museum.

Soundings. El Segundo, CA: AIM.

SuperYacht Times. N.p.: SuperYacht Company.

Thoroughbred Newsletter. Grand Rapids, MI: Century Boat Club.

Waterline. Grand Rapids, MI: Water Wonderland Chapter of the Antique and Classic Boat Society.

WZZM13. Grand Rapids, MI: A Tegna Company.

Yachting. New York: Bonnier Corporation.

INDEX

ABOUT THE AUTHOR

 Geoffrey Reynolds is originally from Charlevoix, Michigan, where he grew up around pleasure craft and grew to appreciate the beauty of area lakes and rivers. He is the Mary Riepma Ross director of the Joint Archives of Holland at Hope College. His research and writing interests are the pleasure and racing boat building industry.

Visit us at
www.historypress.net
....